Knoydart

Knoydart

Denis Rixson

Published by
Birlinn Limited
Unit 8, Canongate Venture
5 New Street
Edinburgh EH8 8BH

ISBN 1 84158 019 8

British Library Cataloguing-in-Publication Data
A Catalogue record of this book is available from the British Library

Typeset by Trinity Typesetting Services, Edinburgh
Printed and bound in Finland by Werner Söderström OY

CONTENTS

FIGURES

MAPS

LIST OF PLATES

INTRODUCTION

Knoydart is a remote and barren peninsula with little recorded history. It lies on the northern edge of what was known in Gaelic as 'na Garbh-Chriochan' - the Rough Bounds – an aptly descriptive term for the area from Moidart to Knoydart (*See* Map 1). Its very name has become something of a byword for 'the Highland problem' – aided by the beauty of its landscape, its desolation and our sentiment. This book attempts to assess what we know or can surmise about its past – and how this informs our present views. It is not a catalogue of every recorded fact about Knoydart. There are long periods for which we know next to nothing and here I have tried to set the history of the area in its wider Highland context. At other times our sources of information are more abundant – as for instance in the eighteenth century. In such cases I have not tried to duplicate the work done by other researchers but have given an overview and a guide to the available material.

My approach is thematic. I have used the various types of evidence – place-names, land-assessment units, sculpture, documentary records and census returns – to unlock the past. Current views about Knoydart depend upon our responses to codewords such as 'Jacobite', 'Clearance', 'emigration' or 'landlord'. They are informed by generations of history-makers who have dwelt on the romance of Bonnie Prince Charlie, the cruelty of the Clearances, the sadness of emigration, the iniquities of landlordism. I am not going to try and pretend any of these away. There is truth in each of these perspectives but equally there are other truths in Highland history which are overshadowed or obscured by our sentimental, and therefore rather distorted, view of the past. We like our history to be leavened by an emotional investment, even if this leaves it unbalanced or incomplete. Our historical understanding helps to shape current political perspectives; in turn our writing of history reflects modern concerns with freedom and equality. For a truer appreciation of Knoydart's history, it is essential to look beyond these partial and contemporary views and try to place the area in its geographical and historical context. Once we do so other truths become available to us.

To modern eyes, tutored by urban landscapes, Knoydart appears beautiful. It is remote, desolate, appealing – and a knowledge of its history lends it an aura of tragedy. If we could go back a thousand years and see it through the eyes of a Norse settler then its beauty becomes less important than its agricultural potential. It was never remote to such a seafarer and its previous history was irrelevant. To a practical colonist, sentiment was self-indulgence. The critical questions were: Is there cultivable land, fresh water, access to the sea, shelter and fuel? By exploring these other approaches we can place our emotional investment in Highland history in a longer, wider context. It is not my intention to reduce the moral intensity with which we approach the politics of landlordism today; but it is my purpose to challenge the relevance of some of our current views when looking at the past. Once we have mourned the loss of a culture, the removal of a people; once we have seen past the individual tragedies, the collective grief; once we have condemned the landlords and cursed the factors; once we have looked beyond the issue of ownership; we still face the problem of self-sufficiency or subsidy.

Since the eighteenth century, the surge in population and expectations have upset an equilibrium that was maintained in Knoydart for thousands of years previously. This balance was not always stable; in years of scarcity, privation had always to be subsidised by theft. The last 250 years have overturned the old relationships between population and resources, in Knoydart as in so many other places in the Highlands. Predation is no longer an option and solutions have usually been imposed from outside. We are left with a sense of tragedy, in terms of individual suffering, in terms of the decline of a whole culture. While the visible effects draw our sympathy, it is important to look beyond these to the underlying causes. What was it about Knoydart society and the nature of the Highland landscape that made it such a victim of change compared to other parts of Scotland? Why did the Highlands not evolve new economic forms as other regions of Britain?

ACKNOWLEDGEMENTS

I should like to thank the staff of Highland Council Library Service for their ready assistance. I am grateful to John Bruce, Norman Newton, Gail Priddice, and in particular to Lorna Skelly of the Library Support Unit for all her patient help in tracing books and references for me. I am also grateful to Nicola Beech of the British Library for her help with the Roy maps and to Dr Jeffrey Stone for his generous advice about Timothy Pont. In addition, my thanks are due to Norman Macdonald (Edinburgh), Alasdair Roberts (Bracara), and Marianne McLean and Ralph Coram (Canada), for help with particular items of information.

I gratefully acknowledge the permission of the Keeper of the Records of Scotland to reproduce the plan of Inveruie Farm (E741/47 f10v).

I am grateful to the Scottish Gaelic Texts Society for permission to quote the English translation of the Dean of Knoydart's poem from W. J. Watson's *Scottish Verse from the Book of the Dean of Lismore*, published by Scottish Academic Press, Edinburgh (1978).

Chapter 1

GEOGRAPHY AND TOPOGRAPHY

Physically, Knoydart appears like an extended knuckle stretching westwards from Loch Quoich. It is bounded on the north by Loch Hourn, on the south by Loch Nevis and to the west by the Sound of Sleat. To the east lie high mountains and the freshwater Loch Quoich. Seton Gordon reports that three cairns beside the track at Mam na Cloich Airde (NM 8994) mark the boundaries of the lands of Lovat (N Morar to the WSW), Lochiel (Loch Arkaig to the ESE) and Glengarry (NE and NW). Since Glengarry held both Knoydart and Glengarry, he was presumably not concerned with the boundary *between* his two territories.

Most of Knoydart is incapable of agriculture. Very little land lies below 200 feet and most of this is confined to the coastal strip and the major glens (*See* Plate 1). Relief has always dictated the district's settlement pattern which concentrated on pockets of land along the coast and in the river valleys of Barrisdale, Guseran, Inverie and Carnach.

Geography has also determined Knoydart's orientation and communications. Access to the east is by steep, rocky passes from Kinloch Hourn, Barrisdale or Carnoch to Loch Quoich, or from Sourlies to Loch Arkaig. These are so harsh and inaccessible as to effectively prohibit commercial traffic through the ages. Men and animals can walk these routes, but little can be carried. Even today only the first of these passes has a road. Knoydart's communications, and therefore orientation, have always been seawards; west to Skye, north across Loch Hourn

1

to Glenelg, or south to Morar. Boats can carry heavy loads and
the distances involved are not great, usually only a mile or two
to Glenelg or North Morar, about three to Skye.

Climate, Soils and Geology

Knoydart's climate is also unfavourable to agriculture. Along
with other parts of the west coast it is affected by the warm-
water currents of the Atlantic Gulf Stream. It enjoys relatively
mild winters, especially on the coast, with a great deal of wet
and windy weather. This favours pastoral, rather than arable,
farming although in past times the climate was not always as it
is now. The Vikings, in particular, enjoyed a climatic optimum
between about 800 and 1200 AD.

Knoydart's natural resources are limited. It has only a tiny
amount of cultivable land, with plenty of rough grazing of varied
quality. It has some woodland but, as we shall see later, this was
not always of economic value. Its rivers support some salmon
and it has peat. It is surrounded on three sides by the sea and
this has always been its richest resource. The underlying rocks,
as for the rest of the Rough Bounds, are an intractable mix of
Moinian schists. The soils are thin, patchy, and heavily leached
by the incessant rain. The only mineral of any value is mica,
which was exploited briefly during the Second World War.

Until the eighteenth century, Knoydart was inhabited on
the basis of agricultural potential alone. There were attempts
by the Forfeited Estates Commissioners to establish a fishing
industry but these ended in failure. It is only in the recent past
that sporting interests, or the desire to have a good view, have
become determinants in settlement. Any historical summary
must reflect this agricultural orientation. People settled here,
not for the mineral resources or the presence of local industry,
not because of strategic ports and harbours or established trade
patterns, but because they could grow crops and graze animals.

Early Topography and Cartography

Our earliest visual impression of Knoydart comes from
Holland. In 1654, Blaeu published Volume 5 of his *Atlas
Novus* and made Scotland one of the best-mapped countries
in the world. In this volume, on a map showing 'Braid-Allaban',

Knoydart appears; not quite as we visualise it today, but with the deep embayment at Inverie instantly recognisable. Kilchoan is marked as a settlement and the glens named at Meadail, Guseran and Barrisdale (*See* Plate 2). Although this map is attributed to Robert Gordon of Straloch, there is good evidence that the groundwork for the western coastline was done by Timothy Pont, the father of Scottish cartography, at the end of the sixteenth century. Pont, minister of Dunnet in Caithness from about 1600, was responsible for the majority of Blaeu's maps of Scotland. He travelled the length and breadth of the country, making sketches and writing descriptions of the areas he surveyed. His motives are not known, although Jeffrey Stone has suggested that it may have been in connection with the newly reformed church in Scotland.

Certainly some of the great statistical and analytical surveys in Scottish history are connected with the Protestant Kirk. Webster's population survey in 1755, the Old and New Statistical Accounts, the collection of 'Moral Statistics' by the Inverness Society for the Education of the Poor in the Highlands in 1822, are all good examples of this appetite for data. Whether it was because the new church needed and wanted the information, or whether it was because ministers were among the few with the education, and the leisure, with which to conduct such investigations, is a matter of almost theological nicety. At any rate, clergymen were always at the forefront of surveys in the Western Isles, from Dean Munro in 1549 to John Walker in 1765 and John Buchanan in the 1780s.

After his death, some of Pont's papers passed to Robert Gordon of Straloch, who had known Pont personally, and thence to Robert's son, James Gordon of Rothiemay. Others among them went to Holland where they became background material for Blaeu's Atlas. There is a collection of his surviving manuscript maps in the National Library of Scotland. Pont not only drew maps, he also made notes of what he saw, as an aide-memoire and to help him in the later process of composition. Not all his original jottings have survived, but in the Sibbald Collections are copies of some of his notes as made by James Gordon. In 1907, Sir Arthur Mitchell edited further copies of these amongst the Macfarlane Papers and pointed out James Gordon's contribution. 'There is no doubt that James Gordon was largely copying when he wrote, but he commented, deleted, and amplified as he copied'. Nevertheless, Mitchell attributed the great bulk of these notes to Timothy Pont, giving them 'exceptional value'. This is an important issue. If the notes which appear in Macfarlane are really Pont's then this makes them the earliest description of Knoydart by at least 100 years. They were probably made between 1583 and 1610 and give us a glimpse of the area as it emerged from the Middle Ages.

Pont's notes survive in two forms, a long and a short version, both of which are printed in Macfarlane. The short version is James Gordon's copy, but bears such a striking resemblance to the long version that it is obvious that they each derive from the same original. It is likely that both Macfarlane versions are later copies of Pont, James Gordon's being contracted and perhaps more polished. (Phrases like 'abundance of milk' become 'abundance of pasture'.) Knoydart is described four times. Two of these are essentially contractions of the other two and so in each case I give the longer, anonymous, version. James Gordon adds virtually no detail and, in the one place he does, his editing is probably an error. (He creates an extra sea-loch in Loch Hourn called Loch-Voirne.)

> Knodeard is a very rough countrey full of mountaines, Glens and sundrie litle rivers wherin is abundance of salmond fish slaine — And in the sea of Knodeord there is abundance of all kind of fish slaine, and bigg mountains on everie syde of this countrie and some of the lands theroff doeth lye southward, some other pairts West and some North forgainst Glenelge, The lands which are in Loghneves forgainst Morrour is rough being the southsyde of the Countrey. The midst of the countrey lyeth westward foregainst Sleit, and this is the most plain and pleasant place of the countrey The Northsyde forgainst Glenelg is verie rough and abundance of salmond fish and herrings and other kynd of fish is slaine in that Logh called Loghuirne, in some little rivers at the syd of the Logh in a glen called Glenbaristill and another river at the head of the Logh And there are great store of deare and rae in Knoidord.

> (Mitchell, A. (ed.), *Macfarlane's Geographical Collections*, *Vol II*, 1907)

(In 1793 Reverend Colin Maciver, Minister of Glenelg, wrote for the *Old Statistical Account* 'The deer and roe still frequent the hills and woods on Lochurn-side'.)

The other description contains some interesting differences:

> this countrey of Knoidort is very fertill of corne, and abundance of milk and all kynd of fishes in this Countrey. There is sundrie litle rivers and speciallie fyve litle rivers. two of them at the head of Loghneves [Carnach & Finiskaig] And there is a bigg mountaine betwixt these two rivers [Sgurr na Ciche] and the river which doeth lye on the Northwestsyde of this high bigg mountaine [Carnach] and it doeth run through a glen and there is abundance of fish in this glen. There are other two Rivers. One of them running through a glen called Meddill. and there is ane fresh water Logh wherthrou another litle river doeth run and there is abundance of fish in this fresh water Logh [Loch an Dubh-Lochain?] and the two waters doe meet togidder and they runn by th parish church of the said Countrie callit Kilghoan and this is the principall dwelling toune of the Superior of that Countrie. And there is abundance of salmond fish slaine in this water of Killhoan, And on the Northsyde of this Countrey there is a verie profitable glen for guids and cattell to feed, And there is a river runneing throwgh this glen And there is abundance of salmond fish slaine therin and this river is called Gaisiron, and the glen is called after that name Glen-gaisiran. There is one Logh of saltwater on the Northsyde of Knoidart, and it goeth farr up above eastward. There is abundance of herrings, salmond and sundrie other fishes slaine in this Logh it is called Loghvoirne. There is one glen at the southestsyde and there is ane litle river or glen therintill. [Barrisdale?]

(Mitchell, A. (ed.), *Macfarlane's Geographical Collections*, Vol II, 1907)

It appears from the above that Pont visited Knoydart twice. The way the notes are laid out suggests that on one of these visits he travelled north by sea since his descriptions move in a geographically coherent manner from Ardnamurchan to Moidart,

Arisaig, Morar and Knoydart. If he landed, he probably only walked as far as Loch an Dubh-Lochain. The fact that he does not give a detailed list of settlements as he does for, say, Trotternish in Skye, suggests he did not spend much time ashore. His description gives the impression of being written by somebody who saw the area by boat; which was, and is, the easiest way to travel.

Proof that the notes really were written by Pont comes in his reference to the 'Superior' of the country living at Inverie. In the immediately preceding section he specifically points out that North Morar belonged to Glengarry – who lived by Loch Oich in the Great Glen. Knoydart did not become Glengarry's until 1611. This is about the time of Pont's death and the fact that he differentiates between the Laird of Glengarry and the Laird of Knoydart establishes that, at the time of writing, these two people were different. This is long before James Gordon made his copy, probably between 1661 and 1686. Gordon made some literary changes, but he evidently did not know enough about the area to edit this much more important fact about ownership.

Assuming then that these notes were written by Pont, can we relate them to the map that appears in Blaeu? In particular, what grounds do we have for ascribing the Knoydart section of Blaeu's map to Pont rather than Gordon of Straloch as indicated on the map itself?

Pont was the source for most of Blaeu's maps of Scotland. This is particularly true of the west coast where Pont is credited with the maps of Kintyre, Knapdale, Lorn, Islay, Jura, Mull, the Small Isles, Skye and Uist. We even have his manuscript maps of South Uist, Loch Linnhe, and parts of the north-west and western coastline as far south as Loch Duich. Blaeu's map of 'Braid-Allaban' etc., though credited to Robert Gordon, is essentially a composite. Blaeu had written in 1642 that his coverage of Scotland was incomplete and specified the areas he was lacking – which included Argyll and Lochaber. Robert Gordon's map was a response to this and since he was already an old man it is likely that he was dependent on Pont's notes and sketches, which he had to hand, for coverage of the west coast. Gordon had probably never seen Knoydart, Pont certainly had.

A characteristic feature of Knoydart, and Blaeu's map, is the deep embayment at Inverie. To anyone approaching by sea this is their first impression, along with the shape of Sgurr na Ciche, which Pont also mentions. Pont must have anchored in Inverie Bay and left some sort of sketch for Gordon whose outline of the coast is otherwise pretty inaccurate. It is also telling that the names that appear in Blaeu match perfectly with Pont's descriptions of the Rough Bounds contained in the Macfarlane Collections. If we include the lands of Moidart, Arisaig, Morar and Knoydart, then exactly the same names occur in the literary and cartographic descriptions, the only exceptions being Lochs Hourn and Nevis which Blaeu omitted. Curiously, these are the very features where Gordon was weakest geographically and makes it feasible that Blaeu also had access to a sketch by Pont which made him doubt Gordon's accuracy in respect of these lochs.

We can understand the nature of Pont's work better if we put it into a contemporary context. The reigns of Elizabeth I in England and James VI & I in Scotland and England saw an explosion of interest in both the wider world and the remoter corners of their own kingdoms. This is the period of the Elizabethan onslaught on Gaelic Ireland, the plantations in Ulster, the colony of Fife Adventurers in Lewis. Ambitious and powerful men dreamt of and pursued fabulous wealth. Alongside the opportunists and adventurers there were also those who had an intellectual interest in the area concerned; those who wished to describe it, map it or assess its economic potential. Such a man was Timothy Pont. We can only admire his stamina and courage. This was a period of bloody clan battles, such as Loch Gruinart between the Macdonalds and Macleans in Islay. This was a time when the Laird of Balcomie, one of the Fife Adventurers, was kidnapped by Murdoch Macleod. This was when Highland fleets travelled to Ireland as mercenaries and engaged with the English off the Copeland Islands. Travelling in the Hebrides was not for the fainthearted and Pont must have enjoyed good relations with at least some of the Highland chiefs. How has his description of Knoydart stood the test of time?

To answer this question we may compare Pont's visual and literary description of Knoydart with its latest image – a satellite photograph (*See* Plate 1). The striking features in the satellite image are the high mountains which show up very white, particularly on their sunlit southern flanks. The freshwater lochs of Bhraomisaig and Dubh-Lochain are well-defined, as are the rivers at Inverie and Inverguseran. The deep embayment at Inverie is obvious and it is apparent that the terrain in the westernmost section of Knoydart, west of a line between Inverguseran and Scottos, is significantly lower-lying. Now let us assess these findings against the earliest descriptions we have of Knoydart – Blaeu's map and Macfarlane's notes – both of which derive from Pont.

The area of the Rough Bounds as portrayed in Blaeu's map of 'Braid-Allaban' is geographically weak. We have the district names of Moidart, Arisaig, Morar and Knoydart, but little other detail. Eilean Tioram is the only site marked in Moidart, Kilmory likewise in Arisaig; no settlements at all are marked in Morar. The alignments north-south are better than those east-west and the whole coastline is only a coarse approximation to reality. Knoydart, however, does surprisingly well. Three of the glens are named. Two of these lead down to the sea and the third, Glen Meadail, is clearly visible from Inverie Bay. The sea-lochs which separate Knoydart from North Morar and Glenelg are also well-defined. The deep embayment at Inverie must have been sketched by Pont for Gordon to include it.

If we turn to Pont's written description, we find he had noted that the 'most plain' (i.e. flattest) part of the country lay facing Sleat, precisely the area that was most densely populated at the time of the Clearance in 1853. Inverie, by Kilchoan, is still the 'principall dwelling toune'; the shores of Loch Hourn and Loch Nevis are yet 'verie rough'. The views of Glen Meadail and Sgurr na Ciche from Loch Nevis are as striking now as they were then. Salmon and deer remain economically important, although for sporting interests rather than as a source of food. Geography does not change greatly and Pont's analysis of the essentials is as telling now as it was when he made it, 400 years ago.

Chapter 2

PREHISTORIC AND EARLY CHRISTIAN

We have very little evidence for prehistoric settlement in Knoydart; this can mean one of two things. Either the evidence does not exist because Knoydart was not populated; or it has not been recognised. The former is inherently unlikely. We have evidence for prehistoric settlement in Skye, Glenelg and Arisaig. Throughout the West Highlands and Hebrides we find cairns and chambered cairns, standing-stones and cup-and-ring marks, kists, crannogs, duns, forts and brochs. These monuments are associated with different phases of the Stone, Bronze and Iron Ages over a period of perhaps 2500 years. It is only to be expected that there will be considerable variation in the distribution patterns of all these classes of monument. Large cairns, for instance, could only be constructed by relatively numerous and settled agricultural populations. The lack of cultivable land in the Rough Bounds meant that this area was always less likely to support such monuments. Kists, standing-stones and cup-and-ring marks are also scarce, but there are several forts and duns. These prove that the Rough Bounds were settled by the Iron Age.

Glenelg has a cluster of fortified sites as well as two exceptionally well-preserved brochs at Dun Telve and Dun Troddan. (A third is said by Leyden to have been demolished and the stones used to build the barracks at Bernera.) Southern Skye is littered with duns, including at least nine between Isle Ornsay and Sleat Point on the coastline facing Knoydart. North and South Morar share Knoydart's archaeological poverty but Arisaig and the neighbouring islands have four forts, a cup-marked stone, a crannog and possibly two cairns. It is unlikely that there are any undiscovered forts, duns or brochs in Knoydart. These structures are usually situated at strategic points and imposing enough to be recognisable. Cairns, though, can be robbed; standing stones toppled, moved or broken up; crannogs submerged; burial kists lost. At first sight Knoydart looks to have almost no prehistoric monuments. They may once have existed in proportion to the area's agricultural value, but have since been hidden from view. The area has been subject to little archaeological investigation. Few roads have been built in Knoydart, and few houses constructed, even today. Peat, moss and bracken swiftly conceal ancient monuments from the casual eye.

If we compare Knoydart with neighbouring areas of land we can put its archaeological legacy into context (See Map 2). With regard to large-scale defensive structures such as brochs, forts, duns and crannogs, which represent a community effort, Knoydart has little to offer. By contrast, Glenelg has at least twelve and Arisaig at least five. Only North and South Morar are poorer. This suggests that, to prehistoric communities, Knoydart had little agricultural value and was unattractive for settlement. We should bear this in mind in the context of later land-valuations. If we take the longer historical view we find that Knoydart was regarded as impoverished by prehistoric, Dark Age, Norse and mediaeval rulers. In later times, our evidence takes the form of low land-values, in prehistoric times we have an absence of communal structures.

North Morar is in a similar situation, seemingly without a single structure earlier than the eighteenth century. However, a number of small circular platforms have recently come to light near Sean-achaidh (Old-field). These are not thought to belong to charcoal-burners. Similar sites elsewhere in Scotland have been dated variously between the Bronze Age and mediaeval times. At the time of discovery the Morar platforms were the furthest north and west of a type with more than 3000 examples. It is most unlikely that North Morar represents a northern boundary for such structures. It may well be that Knoydart has a number of hitherto unrecognised monuments, simply reflecting

the fact that its landscape has escaped the attention of surveyors and the excavations of builders or archaeologists. The mouths of the river valleys at Inverie, Inverguseran and Barrisdale are the most likely locations. Since these were also centres of population in later times, any earlier traces may well have been lost by over-building or stone-robbing. The name Sean-achaidh is recorded in Knoydart in 1637 and may, as in Morar, reflect a much older settlement. To earn the name 'Old-field' in 1637 suggests that we are dealing with a site that is at least mediaeval. At the same time, we must recognise that Knoydart's agricultural poverty argues against either quantity or scale for prehistoric monuments.

Dun Ban

We have one definite prehistoric site in Knoydart – Dun Ban (White Fort) at Doune (NG 701036).The name Doune itself comes from the Gaelic word *dun* meaning fort, of which there are hundreds of examples throughout Scotland. Some, like Dundee, Dunkeld, Dumbarton or Dumfries, became important centres. Others, such as Doune, represent settlements that never grew beyond a cluster of families. Without excavation we have no means of dating this site, though it is likely to be Iron Age in origin and falling within the period 500 BC to 500 AD. It measures about 74 metres by 49 metres and, like the forts in Arisaig, has a heavily vitrified wall. It occupies a strategic site on the coastline facing Sleat (Skye).

The only other site in Knoydart with a possible prehistoric context is an enigmatic mound at Inverie (NM 776991). It is marked on the earliest Ordnance Survey map as the site of a castle, but there is absolutely no evidence to support this. On the contrary, it is noteworthy that there is no record of any castle in Knoydart. At first glance this seems puzzling. We might expect such a large area to support one, although other districts with greater agricultural value, such as Eigg, also lack a castle. In the early mediaeval period Knoydart belonged to the Macruaris and their successors, the Macdonalds of Clanranald. Their headquarters was traditionally Castle Tioram in Moidart which dates from the thirteenth century. The Rough Bounds were too impoverished to support more than one such structure.

After ownership passed to the Macdonells of Glengarry in the early seventeenth century it is understandable that they decided against sustaining two castles, one at either end of their lands. They already had a base at Invergarry on Loch Oich and would be reluctant to invest in Knoydart unless it was necessary. Knoydart was one of many Macdonald estates on the west coast and possibly less prone to external attack. Invergarry lay in the thoroughfare of the Great Glen, close to the lands of several other clans.

As Knoydart became more independent from Clanranald during the fifteenth and sixteenth centuries we might expect some sort of fortified structure at its most important settlement, Inverie. It may well have been wooden. The mound near Kilchoan could represent a prehistoric site, or mediaeval, or both. It consists of a circular turf-covered mound which measures c. 20 metres in diameter and c. 1.5 metres high. There is no trace of a surrounding ditch and bank. Without excavation we can say nothing definite. This is potentially a very important site since it lies at the heart of what was always the most favourable agricultural location in the whole peninsula.

Prior to the arrival of the Norse, c. 800 AD, historians have defined four main cultural groups in Scotland. In the south-eastern corner were Anglian settlers from Northern England. In Strathclyde and the extreme south-west were the Britons, based on Dumbarton. Both of these groups are irrelevant to our current purpose. In Argyll were the Scots from the Kingdom of Dal Riata in Northern Ireland. They had colonised the area from about 500 and by about 800 had established themselves in three well-defined tribal groupings. The tribe of Angus held Islay, Gabran had Kintyre and Loarn occupied Lorn. In the East were the Picts whose territory extended from the Firth of Forth to Orkney and who may themselves have been divided into two groups, North and South.

By comparison with these well-defined cultures there is very little we can say about the north-west. There is almost no recorded history for the area before the arrival of the Norse. We have a few references to the missionary exploits of the early Irish saints but that is virtually all. In the absence of facts the best we can do is make some sensible general observations on

Picts and Scots

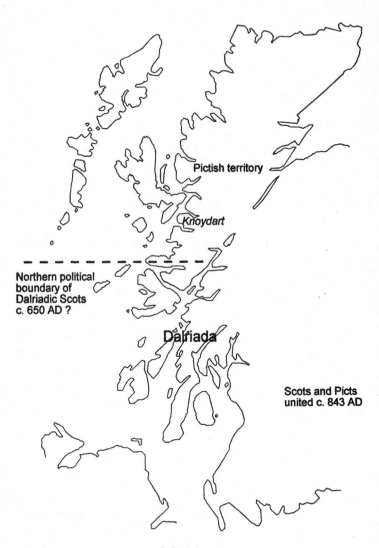

Pictish territory

Knoydart

Northern political
boundary of
Dalriadic Scots
c. 650 AD ?

Dalriada

Scots and Picts
united c. 843 AD

Map 3

the basis of what little evidence does survive.

From their new home in Dalriada the Scots gradually extended their influence eastwards. They eventually overwhelmed the Picts and created the new kingdom of Scotland during the ninth century. They may well have extended their influence north along the west coast but we know absolutely nothing of any political process involved, only something about their religious penetration.

In later centuries Ardnamurchan was regarded as a sort of geographical dividing line; was perhaps even a long-standing northern boundary to Dalriadic expansion (*See* Map 3). This might suggest stable native groups to the north and west who were not easily overwhelmed by the Dalriadic Scots. Or it may simply be that the area was regarded as infertile and unattractive for settlement and expansion, especially when compared to eastern Scotland.

After about 800, the whole of north-west Scotland, mainland and insular, was subject to Norse invasion. Effective political control must have passed to the Norse during the ninth century, but the period between 500 and 800 is largely a mystery. Was the area Pictish, rather than Scottish? Or was it neither, but subject to influences from both? We have evidence from each perspective.

The Pictish Evidence

The neighbouring, and much richer, area of Glenelg may well have been Pictish territory. It dominates the main east-west route between Inverness and Skye, possesses better-quality agricultural land and is seldom more than a mile or two from Knoydart across Loch Hourn. Glen Beag contains two extremely well-constructed brochs in Dun Telve and Dun Troddan. Although these and Dun Grugaig, a semi-broch further up the glen, are pre-Pictish, they argue for a powerful and well-established local dynasty which patronised substantial building projects evolving over many years. Glenelg is almost the only area in the north-west which contains a recognizable *pit* name, viz. Petamain or Pitalman in Glen More. This no longer occurs on the map, but lay between Cnoc Fhionn and Moyle and is probably represented by Bailanailm, where Gaelic *baile* or township has replaced Pictish pett, which meant a piece or portion of land.

Pit-names are associated with Pictish settlement and are

particularly common in eastern Scotland. They also form a convenient marker between two different branches of Celtic language. Little that is recognisably Pictish survives, but the language belonged to the so-called p-Celtic branch and is thought to have been most closely related to Cumbric and Welsh. The other branch, q-Celtic, lacked the p-sound and is today represented by Irish and Scottish Gaelic. At some stage, Glenelg was Pictish rather than Scottish, and it seems reasonable to assume that its immediate neighbour, Knoydart, was also. The problem then arises of when the Pictish language and culture were overwhelmed and absorbed by Scottish Gaelic. Was it before or after the period of Norse colonisation?

In order for a *pit*-name in Glenelg to survive into modern times it is likely that it was in use when the Norse arrived. Norse colonisation destroyed any pre-existing Pictish political system in the north-west. From about the mid-twelfth century there seems to have been something of a Gaelic resurgence, which is associated with the growing power of Somerled's dynasty in Argyll. By the mid-thirteenth century Knoydart was controlled by the Macruari branch of the Macsorleys, and for the rest of the mediaeval period its orientation was towards the Gaelic Lordship of the Isles based on the Macdonalds of Islay.

The situation in Glenelg is different. With Norse conquest it seems to have become a private estate of the Kings of Man. Since their kingdom covered a huge and disparate collection of islands from Man to Lewis it made strategic sense for them to control mainland access to one of their largest islands, Skye. With the ending of Norse control of the Hebrides in 1266, the estate of Glenelg passed to the Macleods, whose power-base lay in Skye and Harris. As a clan they were significantly more Norse than the Macdonalds. Even in the seventeenth century the Macleod poetess Mary Macleod was drawing attention to the Norse roots of her clan

> from the blood of Lochlann's kings thine ancestry
> unbroken takes its rise

and

> from the city of Bergen did thy first title spring.

The Macsorley Estate 1156–1266

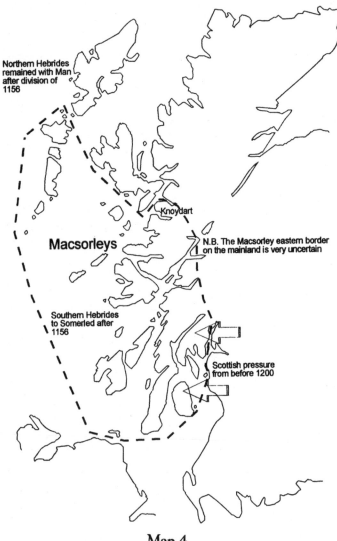

Northern Hebrides
remained with Man
after division of
1156

Knoydart

Macsorleys

N.B. The Macsorley eastern border
on the mainland is very uncertain

Southern Hebrides
to Somerled after
1156

Scottish pressure
from before 1200

Map 4

If Ardnamurchan was a northern boundary to the political world of the Scottish Gael about 650 then this had shifted northwards to lie between Knoydart and Glenelg by about 1156 (*See* Map 4). Of course it did not remain static here. Over the coming centuries a bitter conflict ensued between Macleods and Macdonalds for control of Skye. It would be wrong to see this in racial terms. Over the years the Macleods became as Gaelic in orientation and outlook as the Macdonalds but the political fault-lines that reappear throughout the mediaeval period have their origin in different dynastic backgrounds. The Macdonalds (Macsorleys) were a family who had effectively usurped the power of the Kings of Man over the southern Hebrides. The Macleods represented other equally proud and ancient families in the northern Hebrides, also claiming descent from the royal family of Man.

Land-assessment

Another indication of Knoydart's pre-Norse cultural affinities may be found in its land-assessment units. All land was valued for taxation purposes. These assessment patterns applied from at least Pictish or Dalriadic times, and probably far earlier. This should not surprise us – property taxes such as rates work in a similar fashion. A building has a rateable value – and rates are paid in proportion. In prehistoric, Dark Age and Viking times the land was assessed in terms of its productive capacity and taxed accordingly. (Payment, particularly at the lower levels, was more often in kind than cash.) The legacy of this system is still evident in placenames, charters, and possibly even in estate and farm boundaries.

Both Knoydart and Glenelg use pennylands for the smaller agricultural holdings. Pennylands demonstrate Norse influence because they are subdivisions of ouncelands – that quantity of land reckoned capable of producing an ounce of silver by way of rent. In Orkney and Shetland, the ounceland was worth eighteen pennylands; in the Hebrides and on the west coast it was generally reckoned at twenty. The great estates were parcelled out in ouncelands and these assessments survive in medieval charters. The three terms used in such documents are *unciata* (Latin for ounceland), *davata* (Latin for davach) and *tirung* (Gaelic, literally land-ounce).

Unciata is a direct translation of a Norse, rather than a Pictish or Dalriadic unit. *Davach* was a Gaelic word meaning a 'tub' of produce. It was then applied to the area of land required to render this as tax. The term passed from the Scots to the Picts, presumably at some stage after the sixth century, and came to be widely used throughout Pictland. It survives in place-names as the prefix *Doch–* (e.g. Dochcarty). *Tirung* is a literal translation of ounceland into Gaelic and is much less common. Its use probably developed as Gaelic worked north through the Hebrides during the early middle ages. This process was accelerated by the collapse of the Norse Kingdom of Man after 1263. The Northern Hebrides were used to dealing in ouncelands but the new political authorities were Gaelic-speaking and had their own terminology for land-grants.

Although separate in origin and meaning, the davach came to be regarded as equivalent to the Norse ounceland as the two systems blended together. However, the three names are used rather differently. *Unciata* is perhaps the least specific. It is used in the great land grants to the Macleods and Macruaris, so many ouncelands of Skye or Garmoran — where the individual ouncelands are difficult to pin down. *Davata* is common in charters dealing with properties on the mainland west coast. It is also more specific in that we find definitions of particular davachs of land. Both davach and tirung come from Gaelic, but davach was mediated through the Picts and probably found its way to the north-west coast through their influence. This could have happened at any time between the sixth and the thirteenth century. *Tirung* is most frequently used in the context of the Outer Isles, Coll, Tiree and Northern Skye. It did not apply along the mainland in general, and Knoydart in particular. Davach is used for both Knoydart and Glenelg, and by Lochlan Macruari, Lord of the Rough Bounds, in 1304. Such usage might argue for a Pictish legacy.

The other area in which Pictish influence on the west coast is readily discernible is sculpture. There are six known Pictish symbol stones from the Inner and Outer Hebrides. Three are from Skye, one from Raasay, one from Pabbay (Barra) and one from Benbecula. Five of them bear the symbol of the crescent and V-rod. There are also symbol stones at Gairloch and Poolewe in Wester Ross. Moreover, some of the Early Christian stones in the Small Isles show undoubted Pictish influence, for example a fine cross-slab on Eigg and two crosses from Canna.

Isabel Henderson has argued for the existence of some sort of written record, maintained in Applecross between c. 675 and c. 740. This left its legacy in the form of Pictish entries in the *Annals of Ulster*, a number of which have to do with the Isle of Skye during this period. We have therefore a Pictish agricultural unit in Glenelg, Pictish families and their symbol-stones in and around Skye, and Pictish artistic influence in Eigg and Canna. Taken together these argue for an extensive Pictish presence in the area just north and west of Knoydart both before and after the arrival of Christianity. Unfortunately, it is not yet possible to describe its relationship with the intrusive Dalriadic element.

To the immediate south we are on less certain ground. We have no traces of Pictish influence in Morar, Arisaig or Moidart. It may be that the Rough Bounds formed something of a frontier zone between two cultures. It was a sparsely populated and barren area, north of the main areas of Dalriadic interest and largely beyond the reach of the Picts in their heartlands in Eastern Scotland. It may have been occupied by long-established indigenous peoples who were subject to outside influence, but not overwhelmed, until the arrival of the Vikings. Perhaps they were client or tributary tribes, safeguarded by distance and the poverty of their possessions. The Small Isles were always more accessible than most of the Rough Bounds. They could easily be reached by sea and were free of wolves. In time, Knoydart and the Rough Bounds became part of the Gaelic-speaking world, but not necessarily before the arrival of the Norse. We simply cannot know whether they were Gaelic-speaking by 800, or Pictish, or neither.

Scottish Influence

We must also recognise Scottish influence from Dalriada. Whether or not Ardnamurchan was a political boundary, it was certainly not a religious one. We have evidence of Dalriadic religious infiltration northwards long before the arrival of the Vikings. St Donnan had founded a religious community on Eigg where he and 52 of his monks were massacred in 618 – possibly by a pagan from Arisaig. Becan, the hermit of Rum died in 677. Maelrubha founded Applecross in 673 and died in 722. The comings and goings of numerous Early Christian missionaries argues against any sort of Pictish Iron Curtain. For these Irish missionaries to establish monasteries in favoured sites such as Applecross suggests strong political support from the local rulers. This is unlikely to have occurred if the Dalriadic Scots were seen as intrusive foreigners. Dynastic intermarriage seems a likely avenue of influence, with Irish Christians following Dalriadic princesses northwards. The area north of Ardnamurchan must have been something of a melting-pot between Pict and Scot, an area where the two cultures mingled in what was probably a relatively poor and sparsely populated environment.

Dalriadic religious influence is traceable through Irish monastic chronicles, in place-names, and through carved stones. Any placename bearing the prefix *kil* is associated with these Early Christian missionaries. It is the Irish form of the Latin *cella*, cell or church, and is found throughout the West Highlands and Islands. It is particularly thick in districts like Kintyre, closest to Ireland and therefore most subject to Irish influence. Knoydart has a single *kil*-name, Kilchoan by Inverie which is on record from the sixteenth century. The name Choan refers to St Comgan, a prince of Leinster who left Ireland for Scotland in 717. He settled in Lochalsh where his name survives in the parish name Kilchoan. There are several other Kilchoans in the West Highlands, including one each in Islay and Craignish, one in Ardnamurchan and two in Skye.

Apart from the name Kilchoan we have two graveyards (one of which is early) and a very fine Early Christian carved stone (*See* Plate 3). It is a kite-shaped slab with a cross on each face. On one side is incised a Latin cross with expanded terminals. On the other side is an almost identical cross where the arms are linked by a slightly ovoid disc. Both disc and shaft are elongated in the lower half and the background has been cut away in false relief. The fact that the slab is carved on both sides tells us it was not intended to lie flat on the ground. Equally, its kite shape and elongated lower half implies that the stem was embedded in the earth or a supporting framework of stones. It has Scottish or Dalriadic associations, rather than Pictish, and is comparable with other stones in Argyll. This slab was either a free-standing grave-marker, or a 'termon' or boundary cross. These could be placed at some distance from the church and indicated the extent of its sanctuary.

Sanctuary was an immensely powerful concept in the Dark and Middle Ages. Whatever was within the sanctuary of a church came under ecclesiastical protection. Violation of such sanctuary could have terrible consequences, as suggested by mediaeval cautionary tales. An example from the *Chronicles of Man* describes how Gilcolm, one of Somerled's chieftains, fell foul of St Machutus whilst pillaging in the Isle of Man, and subsequently died a horrible death. The Gaelic name for Applecross is *A' Chomraich* (The Sanctuary) – the confines of which stretched for six miles. There is a fine example of a termon cross still in situ at Kilchoman, Islay – a site dedicated to the same saint as Kilchoan, Knoydart, and where the design of the slab is not greatly different. Unfortunately we cannot yet date these stones very exactly, although in the future a full typology may suggest the most likely time of carving. At present it seems safe to ascribe it to the eighth century and it could be associated with the founding saint himself.

To modern eyes, accustomed to crowded urban graveyards with their innumerable styles of memorial, the grim *momento mori*, the naive trade symbols, the classical urns, the draped and downcast maidens, the military emblems, the broken columns and pilasters, beside all these such rude and simple cross-slabs make little impression. But we must put them in their context. They are the earliest such stones by a factor of several hundred years. When they were first carved, the graveyard contained nothing comparable, at best some wooden crosses. As often as not the community included nobody who could read or write, nobody who built or carved in stone. The contemporary frame of reference was to wooden buildings. Those constructed in stone, such as brochs or duns, were made from unshaped natural boulders and flags. Then suddenly appeared these men, from Pictland or Dalriada, who could execute lasting monuments in carved stone. It is little wonder that the missionary saints enjoyed such prestige in the West Highlands. They were literate, they could build and they could sculpt. Their monuments were durable; in fact many are still with us. Even now the intricate carvings at Applecross, Iona and Ardchattan are impressive. We can only guess at the impact of this superior religious culture on a vulnerable, credulous and superstitious people.

We are left with two distinct cultural blends, a Pictish-Gaelic mix on the mainland, modified by the Norse, and a Norse-Gaelic mix in the islands, with little of any previous culture seeping through. This corresponds with what else we know of the area's early history. The Hebrides were Innsegall or Foreigners Isles, owned by the Norse Kingdom of Man until 1266. The Northern Hebrides were more influenced by the Norse than the Southern Hebrides, and for longer. This may have been partly due to a greater density of settlers and partly because of the success of Somerled's dynasty in Argyll from c. 1150.

We have very little recorded church history for the West Highlands between the Age of the Saints and the medieval period. We know nothing of how Christianity survived during the centuries of Norse occupation. However, there is good evidence that the Norse became Christian relatively early in the Hebrides, certainly long before the first decades of the eleventh century when Norway itself was converted. We know nothing of Knoydart's ecclesiastical history until the fifteenth century. The comments of Presbyterians and later travellers suggest that religious practice in the West Highlands and Islands was primitive, with an undercurrent of paganism. There was a tendency to idolise particular saints, an attitude Protestant commentators found hard to tolerate. Martin Martin reported oblations to a sea-god Shony, and around Loch Maree there were stories of bull-sacrifice. St Comgan was regarded with such veneration by the Highlanders that his image was worshipped. In 1600, shocked Reformers took a wooden statue of the great 'Coan' to Edinburgh where it was referred to as Glengarry's God and burned publicly at the Town Cross.

Chapter 3

KNUT'S FJORD – KNOYDART AND THE NORSE

The nature and degree of Norse settlement on the west coast has been a matter of considerable debate. Nobody doubts they were here – there is an overwhelming amount of circumstantial evidence. The problem is that there is very little that is concrete, no surviving buildings, virtually nothing in the way of archaeological finds. Almost everything is a matter of conjecture – where exactly, when, for how long, how intensively, and in what proportions to the indigenous community? Knoydart was certainly visited by Vikings, its very name means Knut's fjord, but in the absence of material clues we must utilise other forms of evidence.

There is plenty of historical evidence for Norse presence along the west coast. We have the Icelandic sagas, in particular *Orkneyinga Saga*, and the reports of contemporary English and Irish chronicles. We know the Norse occupied some of the mainland as well as the islands. There are references to the men of the 'Dales' who were evidently mainlanders, although the name could apply to districts as far apart as Sutherland or Kintyre. We have accounts of Norse naval expeditions to the islands from the time of Magnus Barelegs in 1098 to the numerous fleets sent in the thirteenth century during the last years of Norse rule. The Norse period lasted from c. 800 to 1266 and it is probable that the earliest phase of colonisation was the most formative. Not once is Knoydart mentioned by name, although the same could be said of virtually the whole of the west coast apart from Kintyre. We have plenty of generalised references in Gaelic history, poetry and folklore, but nothing we can apply specifically to Knoydart. There is also remarkably little archaeological evidence for a Norse presence on the West coast. Most of it applies to the islands – Islay, Colonsay, Coll or Eigg; none of it refers to Knoydart.

In the future, we may construct an architectural typology that lets us chart Norse influence on building traditions in the West Highlands and Islands. In domestic terms there are two distinct forms of building style that can be traced down the centuries – round and long. Neither of these completely ousted the other and there is evidence for both surviving late into the eighteenth century. The ubiquity of rectangular buildings today disguises the fact that until the latter part of the eighteenth century the norm for houses in the Rough Bounds and Lochiel was round. Most inhabitants lived in round creel huts, and had done for hundreds, if not thousands, of years previously. It was only the ruling families who enjoyed better conditions. The tacksmen lived in long, rectangular houses whilst the greatest chiefs had castles. Many of these creel huts may have had a course or two of stonework at the base and many hut foundations lie buried in the bracken fields of deserted Highland settlements. One day these will provide clues to their building ancestry and cultural affiliations.

Our earliest documentary references to Knoydart date to the beginning of the fourteenth century, but they remain bare and infrequent until the seventeenth century. Then, particularly in the Registers of the Privy Council, and usually in the context of some disturbance, we find our first references to places in Knoydart. From here on we are on firmer ground. We can detect real people and actual settlements. In 1637 there is a royal charter to Macleod of Dunvegan which gives a list of Knoydart place-names, along with their land-assessment valuations.

On the basis of such documents, and by analogy with other Highland areas, we can tell a great deal about Norse settlement patterns. The situation continues to improve throughout the eighteenth and nineteenth centuries as we accrue surveyors' reports, rentals, topographical accounts and official census returns. Ironically, the situation in the late twentieth century is beginning to deteriorate again as the native population has almost completely disappeared and is being replaced by English-speaking incomers. The old place-names that were not recorded on maps are vanishing and within a generation will have gone forever.

Documents such as charters and rentals also introduce us to land-assessment units. At first glance this looks dry-as-dust history. A list of place-names with their valuations beside them is as interesting as a list of rateable values today. But, ironically, this is exactly what we are looking at, a list of rateable values, nominally only a few centuries old, but in fact probably dating back to the tenth century, perhaps even earlier. A good deal of work has been done on land-assessment units, and what is extraordinary is how ancient they turn out to be. The standard unit in Knoydart was the pennyland. This dates from Norse times and may overlie earlier Pictish or Dalriadic systems based on davachs and houses, the functional equivalents of ouncelands and pennylands. In turn, these Dark Age systems may themselves superimpose yet earlier assessment patterns. Landforms have not changed greatly over the last 5000 years, even if climate and human occupation have. There is no means by which we can look further than the Norse horizon in Knoydart, but that still gives us a settlement pattern that is nearly a thousand years old, despite the fact that our first evidence for it does not occur until 1637.

Charters and rentals give us place-names, as do early maps and estate surveys. Place-names can reveal a great deal. In terms of their meanings they can tell us something of the economy and society that created them – 'hill of the cow-fold', 'the gravelly beach', 'the mill-stream' etc. In terms of linguistic origin they can tell us the racial and cultural background of their creators. In terms of their survival, longevity and relative importance they tell us something of the pattern and history of settlement.

There has not been a great deal of analysis of personal names in the Highlands but it is realised that these, like place-names, may reveal something of earlier inhabitants. Until quite recently personal names were passed from one generation to the next in a remarkably conservative manner. They often skipped a generation from grandfather to grandson, presumably to avoid confusion, but it is only quite recently that naming-habits have been transformed by the dictates of fashion or taste. It may be that the prevalence of certain personal names and surnames can tell us something of different racial or linguistic origins. Unfortunately, since the indigenous population has now disappeared, we can only do this on the basis of the 1841 census. For the same reasons, studies based on blood types are now irrelevant.

In the absence of any archaeological or documentary evidence for a Norse presence in Knoydart this chapter will concentrate on place-names, personal names and land-assessment units as the most promising sources.

Place-names

Place-name studies are a specialised field, a minefield for those without a background in linguistics. A full analysis of place-name development in Knoydart would require a knowledge of old Norse and Gaelic, and their historical interaction, as well as an assessment of how these names were mediated through Scots or English clerks, cartographers, surveyors and census enumerators. It would have to take into account changes in phonetics, spelling and the inevitable corruption that occurs when a name is misheard, misunderstood or incorrectly translated. For these reasons the following survey is no more than provisional.

Place-name students return to the earliest instance of a name and compare all surviving forms in order to understand the changes that occur over the centuries. We have some isolated seventeenth century references to Knoydart names, and many more from the mid-eighteenth century onwards. Our best single source is a comprehensive list compiled for a charter of 1637. For the most part, these early references only give us the points of settlement. They do not give us the topographical features which generally escaped attention until they were mapped by Ordnance Survey officers in the late nineteenth century. This does not make such settlement lists any less valid. From a landowner's point of view, occupation sites were always the most important features in a district. These provided his resources of men, money and food. However, it does mean that when looking for signs of Norse influence we are looking at settlement names rather than topographical features.

How were these charter lists compiled? By a scribe, usually in a Lowland context, transcribing a list of names provided by someone with local knowledge. In many cases this may have been the landowner himself, whose primary interest lay in the settlement sites and not the topographical features, except insofar as they defined boundaries. We can be sure that places named in such a list represent settlements, less sure that they are a faithful representation of the local linguistic mix. Some of them may represent old strata of settlement and are a relic of the previous occupants.

There are several types or classes of Norse name, and there has been a good deal of debate about the relative weightings to attach to these. A purist might argue that only when you find 'habitative' names such as –bol (farm), or –setr (dwelling) can you prove Norse settlement. Anything else, particularly names with topographical elements such as –dalr (valley), –fjall (hill), and –aig (bay) just demonstrate Norse influence. From a minimalist point of view these might only indicate seasonal visits from Norse colonies in the Hebrides.

Against this it has been argued that in other areas of proven Norse settlement, such as Iceland, topographical names are given to habitation sites. Why should the same not apply in Knoydart? This argument cannot be resolved since the absence of Norse settlement names will always leave some doubt about the nature of their occupation. However, if we consider the sheer *quantity* of Norse names, the distances they stretch inland, and their influence on Gaelic naming practice, we can be in no doubt that the west coast, including Knoydart, was extensively colonised by Norsemen. When, for how long, and in what proportions to the indigenous population remain a matter for debate.

Knoydart falls into the expected zone of Norse settlement. The Norse colonised the Hebrides extensively; in fact, the islands were known to Gaelic-speakers as Innse Gall or the Foreigners Isles. The border between Norse and Pict was never the coastline but the watershed to the East. The Norse were sea-oriented. They would settle the coastal strip and the hinterland that drained into it. They would not stray the other side of the mountain barrier.

Figure 1: Knoydart's Settlements

No	Value (1d)	1637 charter	Modern Name	Canada list	Census Returns
1			Kinloch Hourn	Ceanlochourna	Lochourn Head
2	½d	Sky	Skiary	Sciaarie	Skiary
3			Runival	Ruonabal	Runival (1891)
4			Camusnacrogan (KP)	Camasnacroggag	
5			Caolisbeg (KP)	Kilesbeag	
6	2½d	Barrastoll	Barrisdale	Barastal	Kylesmore*
7			Inbhir Dhorrcail	Inerghortcail	Barrisdale
8			Muinal (KP)	Muneal	Inverghorkill
9	1d	Cokisdoyne	Camas Domhain		Muineal
10	2d	Lie	Li	Lee	Lee
11			Glac nan Sgadan	Glaicnascaddan	Glacnasgadan
12	1d	Scaimadoll	Scamadale	Scamadal	
13	2d	Crolin	Croulin	Kroling/Krolig	Crowlich
14	2d	Ardnaslisheniche	Ard Slisneach	Ardnaslishnich	
15	5d	Innergeisarrone	Inverguseran	Inerghaesherain	Inverguseran
16	1d	Nisgart	Niag-ard	Niargart	Neagart
17	1d	Auchnahuiche	? Leachdnahishe		
18	1d	Sandland	Samadalan	Samadalan	Samadlan
19	2d	Torrarie	Torr-airigh		
20	2d	Hirramarie	Aitor?		
21			Doune	Errar	Earar
22	2d	Tilliefair	Telesaig	Dunn	Dun
23	2d (5d)	Sandaig	Sandaig	Teleseg	Tellisaig
24	1d	Riddarrache	Reidh an Daraich	Sandaig	Sandaig
25	½d	Glaschoil	Glaschoille	Ridarach	Radaroch
26	5d	Scuto	Scottas	Glaschoile	Glaschoille
27	1d	Muneroy	? Inverie (veag)	Scotas	Scottos
28	2d	Ristermemeroy	? Inverie (more)	Ineraibheg	
29	5d	Gillichoane	Kilchoan	Ineraimhore	Inverie?
30	5d	Senachadische	Seanachaidh	Killechomhain	Kilchoan
31	1d	Millarie	Miol-airighe	Shennachagh	Shenachy
32	2d	Glenducachone	Gleann an Dubh-Lochain	Mialarie	
				Glendulochan	Glendulochan

#			(Kinlochdubhlochain)	Ceanlochadulochain	Glenmeddle
33			Mam Barrisdale	Mam Bharastail	Glenmeddle
34			Gleann Meadail	Glennmeddle	
35			(Scottary)	Scautary	
36			Bun an Cnap	Bunnachnaip	
37			Gorten a gobhar	Gortainnagoar	
38					
39	½d	Grob	Grob	Grob	
40	1d	Rigerall (or Rigwall)	Reidh a Ghuail	Righuil	Righuil
41	1d	Braonsaick	Braomisaig	Bruiseg	
42	1d	Salacharrie	Salachairigh	Salacharie	Salachary
43	1d	Kelist	Kylesknoydart	Kiles Knodarrach	Kyles
44	½d	Torocund	Torr Cruinn	Torrcruinn	Tocrine
45			Camusrory		Camusrory
46	1d	Granoche (or Garnoche)	Carnoch	Charnach	Carnoch
47	1d	Forgus	Sourlies	Soarchas	Sorhes
48	1d	Gorken	Gorten		
49	½d	Achaglyn	Achaglyne	Achaglinna	
50	½d	Garsline	Garsley		
51	½d	Bragahadische	Breacachaidh		
52	½d	Turnebrusche	(Torr) na Bruaiche		
53			Cluain-airighe		Claonary

Total 56 ½d (60d)

* Kylesmore is probably meant to be Kylesbeag. Except for Runival the Census List is composed from the 1841 and 1851 returns.
At the eastern extremity of Knoydart I have omitted Loan, Aultfern, Glen Cosaidh and Coireshubh. In Western Knoydart I have left out Satial, Folach and Aultvoulin. In all these cases the settlements were either late, secondary or very small. Neither have I included Dale, a clear Norse name, which appears beside Inverie in a rental of 1802 – and is definitely not Meadail. For the 1637 charter I have worked from a printed version. The Canadian lists and the Census Returns are in manuscript form so there is plenty of scope for misreading and error.
All spellings should be treated with caution.
Breacachaidh, and several similar names in the Highlands and Islands, includes as a first element a word that has been derived from Gaelic *breac* (speckled) or Norse *brekkr* (slope). In the case of Bracara (North Morar) and perhaps Breacachaidh (Knoydart) it may come from the Norse.

Conclusions

I have underlined the names in the 1637 Charter and the Canadian list which include Norse elements. These represent 43% (Canada), 35% (Charter) or 37.5% (by pennyland valuation) of the respective totals. The settlement names represent a substantial Norse input.

It is doubtful that the Norse were ever in a numerical majority
on the coastal mainland. They arrived c. 800 in an area that was
probably only sparsely populated. Over the next 450 years they
settled extensively. They may have come in waves or sporadically,
rather than in a continuous stream and there was probably more
colonisation in the earlier period than the later. The rise of
Somerled's family in Argyll in the first half of the twelfth century
initiated something of a Gaelic political resurgence. Certainly it
meant that new Norse migrants could not just help themselves
to land in Argyll and the Southern Hebrides. Local political
control was not challenged by the Norse after Somerled's day.
The main period of settlement was over well before 1150 and the
Norse who colonised Knoydart probably did so between 850 and
the death of Thorfinn of Orkney c. 1065.

The only clues we have lie in the relative proportions of
surviving Gaelic and Norse place-names, and possibly in personal
names. The Norse may only have accounted for a powerful
minority in the local population. However, since their families
exercised political control over a long period, and since it was
their families, now Gaelicized, who provided property lists to
the clerks who wrote the medieval charters, so it is their names
that have survived. Any local Gaelic population of the tenth
century may have had quite other names for settlements we
now only know in Norse terms. The fact that the latter survived
whereas the former did not does not necessarily indicate that
there were more Norse than Gaels, simply that they were more
powerful.

In order to see how much the Norse contributed to the
settlement pattern of Knoydart we need the earliest possible list
of inhabited settlements. This is provided by a charter of 1637
to Macleod of Dunvegan. Because this is not quite complete,
and in order to provide cross-references, I have ranged it beside
two other early lists (*See* Figure 1). One was compiled in Canada,
perhaps in the middle of the nineteenth century, and comes from
the papers of Father Ewen John Macdonald. Father John left
Knoydart in 1786 as a boy of four and so presumably composed
his list from information supplied by older relatives amongst the
emigrants. He actually left two lists, one substantially longer
than the other, which I have conflated for this account.

These were compiled in a geographically coherent manner, running anti-clockwise round the coast of Knoydart from Kinlochhourn, exactly as the charter of 1637. Despite being nineteenth-century in their present form, these lists are essentially a record of the situation when the emigrants left in 1786. It is striking that the names are overwhelmingly those of coastal settlements, they do not include topographical features, and show very few settlements inland.

The final list is drawn from the nineteenth century census returns. These are not completely reliable. Sometimes the enumerator ran neighbouring settlements together and included them under one heading, presumably to save himself work. By 1841, the earliest census to specify place-names, it was also the case that some settlements were abandoned or only occupied sporadically, for instance by shepherds. The final column in Figure 1 is therefore something of a composite of different census returns. Nevertheless, between them these three lists give a pretty clear picture of the past settlement pattern in Knoydart. About a third of the settlement names are wholly Norse (Scamadale, Li), or include a Norse-derived element (Inverie, Telesaig, Salachairigh).

How do we know that names are Norse or Norse-influenced? Clues are provided by what they named and how they named. The former avenue is less productive; both Gaels and the Norse occupied the same environment and their names reflect similar concerns about the local topography. However, it may be that further study will reveal differing proportions between the types of feature named in either language. Fortunately, they had different *methods* of naming, differences which are now invaluable for detecting the influence of one or other culture. The Gaelic process is general (generic) followed by particular (specific), e.g. Ben More (hill big) or Glen Beag (valley small). In Norse names the process is reversed, e.g. Scamadale (short dale) or Langwell (long field). If therefore we find a generic at the end of a word, even if it has all the appearance of being Gaelic, this indicates Norse influence. For example the word for a shieling or summer pasture is *airigh* (Gaelic) or *erg* (Norse), the Norse having borrowed it from the Gaels at an early stage. Following the rules of word order outlined above, we can tell something of a name's origin depending on whether we find this element first or last. The former, as in Arinagour (Coll), indicates Gaelic influence, the latter, as in Scottary (Knoydart), suggests Norse. In Norway itself, and some places in the Scottish islands, the word used would have been *saettr*.

A further feature of Norse influence is name-inversion. This occurs when the expected word order is reversed. In Gaelic, the word Ben (hill) comes before the descriptive term, More (big), Beag (little) etc. Within the Rough Bounds the normal word order is frequently reversed, suggesting that the Gaelic naming process was modified by Norse influence. Examples of name-inversion in Knoydart include the two biggest hills, Luinne Bheinn and Ladhar Bheinn, as well as Slat Bheinn by Glen Barrisdale.

There are no convincing 'habitative' names with endings in *-bol* or *-setr* which could prove settlement. However, there are two names which come close to it. Our earliest spelling of Samadalan is actually Sandland (1637). If this is correct then both elements are Norse, meaning exactly as they do in English. *Land* is a fairly common element in farm names in the far North of Scotland (Merkland, Greenland) and is also found in Glenelg (Suardalan) and North Morar (Swordland). Sandland may therefore indicate the site of a Norse colonist's farm. More likely still is the name Miolary near Inverie. Miol occurs in Gairloch and, with the ending *-ary* or shieling, in Knoydart and Glenelg. In Gairloch it is a contraction of *mjo-vollr* (literally narrow field). *Vollr* is a common farm-name element in the north of Scotland and also down the entire west coast as far as Kintyre and Bute. It usually appears as the suffix *-well*, *-wall* or *-al*. Common forms are Langwell (long-field), Braal (Broad-field) and Rossal (Horse-field). In Moidart, we have Langal which is a variation of Langwell.

Almost all other Norse names in Knoydart are topographical (i.e. to do with landscape features). They fall into several groups. One category includes *-dalr* (dale or valley) which is extremely common along the whole west coast. In Knoydart, we have Barrisdale, Meddail and Scamadale. The last is pure Norse and illustrates their very practical approach to naming. It literally means short dale, which is exactly what it is. Scamadale is also a good example of how the same names recur down the west coast and particularly through the Rough Bounds. There is a Scamadale off Loch Shiel, another off Loch Morar, one in Knoydart and one in Glenelg. Unndalainn is more doubtful but could derive from *eng* (narrow) and *dalr*, which again is very descriptive. There is another Undalain in Glenelg which is similar geographically, as well as Gleann Udalain in Lochalsh.

Another group consists of those names ending in *-aig*, which derives from *-vik* (a bay). These include Sandaig, Braomisaig, Telesaig. A third group are the *-ary* or shieling names which include Skiary, Torrary, Scottary, Cluanary and Miolary. There are also single Norse words which serve as free-standing names even today: Li (from *hlidh*, a cliff or slope), Airor (possibly from *eyrar*, a gravelly beach). Runival is the only name where the Norse word *fjall* or hill has survived, elsewhere it has been replaced by the Gaelic Beinn.

The principal settlement in Knoydart is Inverie, for which we have an early Gaelic spelling in the poetry of Alasdair Macdonald. In a poem about his new home, composed sometime after 1751, he spells the word *Ionbhar* (Inver)-*Aoidh*. Here, the second element is the Gaelic version of the Norse word *eid* which means a narrow isthmus or neck of land – a term frequently used in the Northern Isles. It also survives in the Eye peninsula off Stornoway which is connected by a narrow landbridge known as the Aoidh. The word has the associated sense of being a crossing-point between two stretches of water. In the days of sailing-ships, boats and cargoes could be held up for weeks by contrary winds. In some places either the boats were hauled across or the goods were unloaded on one side and carried by land to the other, from where they continued by water. This practice of portage was common throughout Europe in the past.

The equivalent word to *eid* in Gaelic is *tairbeart*, as in Tarbert, Loch Fyne, which to the Norse was known as *Satiris-Eid*. The word *eid*, *aoidh* or *uidh* survived in Gaelic alongside *tairbeart* and occurs in place-names on the west coast from Cowal northwards. It has been argued that some of these Tarberts, as for instance from Loch Sunart to Loch Linnhe, were far too long for boats to have been portaged. Practice probably varied greatly. There is no doubt that by Loch Fyne, Loch Lomond and Loch Morar, where the distances were short, boats could be and were hauled across. In other cases the cargoes were unloaded but the same name, by a process of association, was given to natural passes which linked two stretches of water. So in Knoydart we can imagine the *aoidh* was the natural route between Loch Nevis and Loch Hourn. This would be used for communication and commercial traffic and was probably an ancient thoroughfare for communities on either loch. Inverie was the *inbhir* or mouth of the *aoidh*, and the name then attached to the river. Confirmation of this process is found in the Forfeited Estates Papers where the river is referred to as the 'Water of Uie' and the name Inverie is consistently spelled Inveruie (*See* Plate 7). Another example occurs in Glenelg where the natural pass between the head of Glen Beag and the head of Glen Dubh Lochain is called Glen Aoidhdailean.

Personal Names

It has been suggested that the occurrence of particular personal or surnames may help indicate cultural origins. Names like Ranald or Torquil, Macaulay or Maciver, are Norse in origin and their frequency may betray the settlement patterns of the original settlers. This is an inexact science, not least because surnames are relatively recent on the west coast. The seventeenth century Privy Council records describe individuals from Knoydart with a string of patronymics such as *Martine McEane VcRorie VcEane Roy*. By the nineteenth century, surnames were becoming fixed, but even in the census returns there was variation. It is perfectly possible to find somebody described as Macdonald in one census return, Macdonell in the next. Of course these are really just the same name, the former more anglicised than the latter, but it shows that surnames have to be treated with caution. The 1851 census gives us a complete list of Knoydart's inhabitants.

What does such a list reveal? If anything it reveals an absence of Norse influence. The surnames are almost exclusively Gaelic. The eight most common surnames: Macdonald, Mackinnon, Macpherson, Cameron, Kennedy, Macdougall and Campbell together account for over 71% of all names in 1851. Of these, only Macdougall (son of Dubh-Gall or black-stranger) has even

Knoydart's pennyland assessment

On 13 March 1637, King Charles I gave John Macleod of Dunvegan a charter for the lands of Knoydart. This can be found in the Register of the Great Seal, Vol IX No 677. (This charter had no political effect and arose simply because Macleod had acted as security in a debt Glengarry had incurred). The charter lists 56 ½ pennylands out of Knoydart's total of 60. In a rental of 1762, Kinlochhourn appears as 1d and Sandaig as 5d rather than 2d. If Kinlochhourn included the assessment for Skiary then these adjustments bring the total to 60d.

One or two anomalies remain. In 1798, Caolasbeg, (between Barrisdale and Skiary), appears as a ¼d. I have indicated its position on the map but have not included it within the total since I suspect it was a late subdivision of Barrisdale. As population grew it may be that fragmentation of the old pennyland units became common. The half-penny (*leth-peighinn*) and farthing (*feorlin*) were also used to describe land-units and occur in place-names such as Lephenstra and Feorlindubh. Caolasbeg's value indicates that even further subdivision took place. Two of Knoydart's original pennylands survive in the names Penvoit and Penvoir which Fraser-Mackintosh noted at Glendulochan.

Fortunately the lists runs in a geographically coherent fashion which makes the identification of most names quite straightforward (*See* Figure 1). This is often the case in charters and suggests that the clerk copied from someone who had local knowledge and worked through the settlements in a logical manner. The list starts with Skiary near the head of Loch Hourn and then runs anti-clockwise around Knoydart to the head of Loch Nevis. The last three names on the list are out of order. The first two of these, certainly, and the third, probably, are small settlements up Glen Guseran. The names which present difficulty are Auchnahuiche, Hirramarie, Muneroy, Risternemeroy and Turnebrusche. The first is probably near Leachdnahishe (now Leathad Mor) on the north-east side of Glen Guseran. Hirramarie sounds as if it derives from Airor. Muneroy and Risternemeroy were probably by Inverie whilst Turnebrusche is possibly Torr na Bruaiche, off Abhainn Bheag up Glen Guseran.

What does the pennyland map reveal? Firstly that settlement was overwhelmingly coastal. There are few inland settlements and they are all up the river valleys of Inverie, Guseran and Carnach. The south shore of Loch Hourn (from Crowlin to Kinlochhourn) and the north shore of Loch Nevis (from Groab to Sourlies) together amount to less than a third of the total valuation. Even in Norse times the two main areas of settlement were the western coastal strip from Ardnaslishnish to Sandaig and around Inverie Bay. It is likely that the Norse settlement pattern itself overlay a previous Pictish one. The names are a real linguistic mix but despite the presence of four 5d units it is noticeable that there are no *Kerr*-names in Knoydart.

Knoydart amounted to 3 ouncelands or davachs and knowing this we can compare it with other areas in the Highlands and Islands. Glenelg was 12 ouncelands, Eigg 5, Muck and Rum 1 each. North Morar was only 12d, not even 1 ounceland. Despite its size, Knoydart was regarded as poor. This Norse assessment persisted into Scottish times when the ratings were in merklands. Ouncelands were translated into merklands, first of all in an 'Old Extent' conducted in the thirteenth century and then in a 'New Extent' in the fifteenth century. In Kintyre the conversion rate could be up to 1 ounceland to 10 merklands (Old Extent). In Knoydart, it was reckoned as low as 1 to 1 (Old Extent) or 1 to 5 (New Extent). If Knoydart was poor to the Norse, it was practically worthless to the Scots.

the remotest Scandinavian connection. We simply do not find names like Macaulay, Macaskill or Macsween which are Gaelic versions of the Scandinavian personal names Olaf, Asketil and Svein respectively. Having said that, surnames must be treated with caution. They were adopted late and in many cases may derive from an allegiance to, rather than a strict line of descent from, the Macdonells of Glengarry. The fact that 37% of the people of Knoydart in 1851 are called Macdonald or Macdonell does not mean they all descended from Donald of Islay (d. c. 1250). It may simply mean that many took on the surname of the family they were associated with, related to, or felt allegiance towards. In other Macdonald areas such as Morar and Arisaig, old names like Maclellan and Maceachan survive. The situation is more ambiguous in Knoydart.

What about first names? Here also we are struggling. None of the popular male or female personal names is demonstrably Norse, although there are a few instances of Lachlan (from Lochlann, Norway) and Ranald or Ronald (from Rognvald).

The evidence from personal names is broadly negative but we should recognise that personal names are necessarily subject to greater change than place-names. Christian names evolve with every generation and over a period of time it is inevitable that the number of Norse personal names would reduce. Surnames have only become fixed in recent times and are a much less certain indicator of background. It appears that the Norse presence in Knoydart, as indicated by personal names, was completely overwhelmed by a process of Gaelicization long before the first census return in 1841. Since then, of course, the indigenous population has disappeared from the district. In other areas, such as Skye and Lewis, the Norse legacy in personal names is much stronger, despite many centuries of Gaelic domination.

Land-assessment
Another aspect of Norse colonisation which is very revealing is the issue of land-assessment. We know that the whole of Knoydart amounted to three ouncelands (or davachs) which were divided into 60 pennylands (*See* Map 5). Pennylands are found all the way down the west coast, thicker in some areas than others, and as far inland as Glengarry. The Orkney Earldom

was dominant in the area between about 980 and 1065 and the pennyland system probably resulted from their fiscal organisation of the Hebridean colonies. The reason for associating pennylands with the earlier period of Norse colonisation rather than the Kingdom of Man (after 1079) or Somerled's dynasty (after 1156) is that they are also found in Carrick and Galloway. Neither of these areas was ever part of the Kingdom of Man or the Lordship of the Isles. Similarly, we cannot associate them with the Macsorley dominion because we also find them in islands of the Northern Hebrides which were controlled by other families.

An intriguing feature of Knoydart's pennyland distribution is the occurrence of four 5d units at Inverguseran, Sandaig, Scottos and Kilchoan. In the Hebrides and along the west coast, a 5d unit was a quarter-ounceland (or quarterland) and matched with a ceatramh, the equivalent fraction of a davach. These subdivisions are commonly recorded in place-names beginning with Ker- or Kirrie- and were important estates in themselves. Some have argued that the quarterland corresponded to a Norse unit called the *manngerd* or *lide* which was responsible for providing one man for naval service. The West Highland evidence is too inconsistent to be sure of whether a similar relationship existed here, but it is possible. Certainly in 1304 Lochlan Macruari, lord of the Rough Bounds, ordered each davach of land to furnish a galley of twenty oars. This was probably ambitious because it is difficult to imagine the three davachs of Knoydart sustaining three galleys and their crews – a total of at least 66 men. The whole population of Knoydart may only have been a few hundred, of whom over half would have been female.

Conclusion

It seems likely that there was a significant Norse racial and linguistic input in Knoydart. From the ninth to the twelfth century the Norse owned or had political control over the area, subjugating a sparse local population that was Pictish or Gaelic or both, and naming some of the principal settlements in their own terms. Then, either because of Gaelic resurgence, or because their own numbers were small and unsustained by fresh waves of migration, they were absorbed into the indigenous population which was, or became, Gaelic by the thirteenth century. Here we are in the murky waters of supposition rather than fact. How, and over what period of time the process took place is completely conjectural. It is likely that Norse colonists occupied some of the principal settlement sites such as Barrisdale, Sandland, Sandaig and Inverie. Over the generations they intermarried with local families and dynasties, thus helping to legitimise their own position. They renamed the principal occupation sites in their own terms. Unless such names had been accepted and perpetuated locally they would not have survived into the fourteenth century when they were passed to the clerks who enshrined them in charters.

The district names for the Rough Bounds, which are our earliest place-names for this area, are predominantly Norse: Knoydart, Arisaig, Moidart, Sunart. They would not have been passed to the royal clerks unless they had legitimacy in the eyes of the estate owners, the Macruaris, a branch of Somerled's family. The Macruaris were the most pro-Norse of all the Macsorleys and fought a rearguard action against Scotland after Hakon's failed invasion of 1263. Knoydart was owned by a family who were frequently present at the court of the Norwegian kings, who accompanied them on their campaigns to Denmark, who served on boats in the Norwegian fleet and who sometimes married Norwegians. Although active Norse colonisation may have ended 200 years earlier, Knoydart was sufficiently well-connected to the Scandinavian world for Norse place-names to survive into a culture that was increasingly Gaelic.

It was not necessarily a question of Norse conquest and Gaelic reconquest. If anything, this would make Norse names less likely to survive. It is more likely to have been a gradual process of integration as powerful incomers, who could always call on reinforcements from the Hebrides, were gradually absorbed by, and integrated with, a numerically larger local population. Contemporaries were well aware of this process. Tenth century writers talk of the Gall-Gaidhil, the 'foreign-Gaels' of mixed Norse-Gaelic descent who occupied the Hebrides and who, according to the Irish chroniclers, were more ferocious than the Vikings themselves. From these distinct

Chapter 4

KNOYDART IN THE EARLY MIDDLE AGES

We know very little of Knoydart in the medieval period. Its remoteness and poverty meant it was always on the periphery of events. However, we can say something of its political history from the twelfth century, and we have a poem and some carved stones to help us glimpse its cultural life in the fifteenth and sixteenth centuries.

The political framework
Norse political control of the Hebrides ceased in 1266. Hakon's invasion of 1263 was the last attempt by the Norwegian monarchy to retain the islands. Though not defeated in battle, his fleet failed to overawe the Scots who knew that time and geography were on their side. In the absence of annual support from Norway, the chiefs of the Western Isles had to make their own terms with Scotland, and in 1266 the islands were formally ceded by the Treaty of Perth. Knoydart had always been Scottish in name, but in practice was controlled by the Macsorleys whose power-base lay in Argyll and the southern Hebrides. The family of Somerled had emerged in the mid-twelfth century to control much of mainland Argyll. Somerled's wife, Ragnhildis, was of the royal house of Man, but in 1156 Somerled defeated Godred, King of Man, in battle and assumed control of the Southern Hebrides. It is likely that his mainland estate included Knoydart, though how or from whom he acquired it we have no idea.

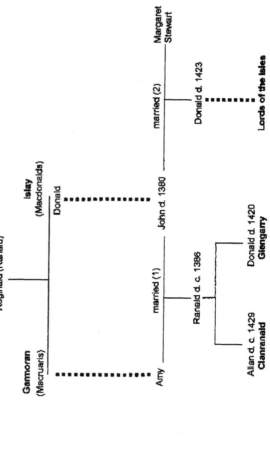

Figure 2: The Macsorleys

Fragmentation of the Macruari Estate

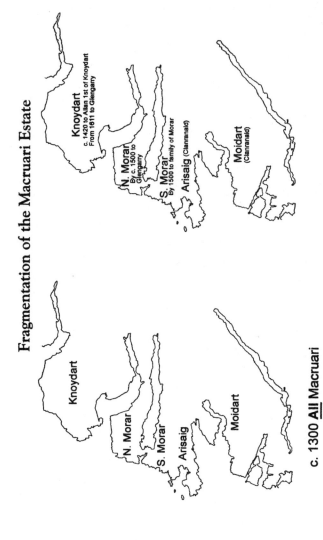

Knoydart
c. 1420 to Allan 1st of Knoydart
From 1611 to Glengarry

N. Morar
By c. 1500 to
Glengarry

S. Morar
By 1500 to family of Morar

Arisaig (Clanranald)

Moidart
(Clanranald)

Knoydart

N. Morar

S. Morar

Arisaig

Moidart

c. 1300 **All** Macruari

Map 6

Somerled himself was unacceptable to the island chiefs who owed allegiance to the King of Man. His sons, however, could claim legitimacy through their mother and under them a Lordship of the Isles became established, first in practice and then in name. After Somerled's death in 1164 his house divided into three, each taking different parts of his huge estate. His mainland possessions fell largely to Dugall, whose family, the Macdougalls of Lorn, were dominant in the area until the Wars of Independence and their defeat by Bruce about 1309. Islay went to Donald, whilst the family of Ruari were established first in Kintyre and later in the Rough Bounds at the northern edge of Somerled's territory.

In 1337, Amy Macruari married her distant cousin John of Islay (*See* Figure 2). When her brother Ranald was murdered in 1346, the Macruari estates fell to her and so to her husband John. In this way the lands of two branches of the Macsorleys were reunited. The mainland Macruari estates then passed to Ranald, son of John and Amy. When he died c. 1386 these lands were divided between his sons, principally Allan and Donald, who founded the Clanranald and Glengarry families respectively. Knoydart appears to have belonged to Allan. After his death c. 1429, Knoydart passed to his second son, another Allan. His line continued until c. 1613 when it was suppressed by their relatives from Glengarry. Knoydart then passed to the Glengarry family until it was finally sold outside Clan Donald in 1857 (*See* Map 6).

Looked at in its overall geopolitical context, Knoydart was a Macsorley estate between c. 1150 and 1857. For 700 years it was firmly linked to the fortunes of the Macruari, Clanranald or Glengarry branches of Somerled's kindred. The men of Knoydart participated in the Macdonald wars, without necessarily sharing all the Macdonald misfortunes. Islay and Kintyre might pass to the Campbells of Argyll; Knoydart was too far north to fall under their effective control.

The mainland province of the Macruaris and then the Macdonalds of Clanranald was the area between Loch Shiel and Loch Hourn. This huge estate was known historically as Garmoran, or by the apt Gaelic description 'na Garbh Chriochan' – the 'Rough Bounds'. These included the distinct districts of

Moidart, Arisaig, North and South Morar, and Knoydart. That Loch Hourn, and therefore Knoydart, was on their northern frontier is indicated by lines in a satire on Allan Macdonald of Clanranald who died c. 1509. The author was Finlay, the Red Bard, and he refers to the people of Clanranald inhabiting the lands between 'Seile and Subhairne'. W. J. Watson, the editor of the *Book of the Dean of Lismore*, regarded the second name as a rendering of Loch Hourn and drew attention to Coire Shubh, up from the head of the loch.

The next peninsula to the north is Glenelg, which traditionally belonged to the kings of Man, from whom it passed to the Macleods of Harris and Dunvegan. Over a period of centuries the Macleods fought a rearguard action against the northern expansion of Somerled's family. The Macsorleys were originally established in Argyll and the southern Hebrides. With the acquisition of feudal power in the earldom of Ross after 1437 they leapt north. The southern limit of the Manx-controlled northern portion of the old kingdom of Man seems to be represented by the Macleod territories of Glenelg, Skye and Harris. Knoydart was something of a frontier province. Its relative poverty and sparse population meant that it posed no threat to its northern neighbour, Glenelg. Equally, any who raided in Knoydart would know that they had the whole of Clanranald to deal with – an undoubted disincentive. It is noticeable that for several centuries Knoydart represented a stable frontier – in marked contrast to the situation in Skye.

The Macruaris

The Macruaris are the most shadowy of the three great offshoots of Somerled's family. They seem to have been displaced from Kintyre, perhaps in the early thirteenth century, and from their new power-base in Garmoran they adopted a very pro-Norse position. They were robust supporters of the Kings of Norway both before and after the invasion of 1263. In 1264 Dugald Macruari defied a Scots punishment expedition that reduced Caithness, Ross and Sutherland and at least threatened Skye. We are told that 'Lord Dugald defended himself in ships, and they took no hold of him'. The Macruari lords eventually came to terms with the Scottish realm but their remoteness made them virtually impossible to control. They were inaccessible to land attack and their power derived from their galleys which were unchallenged in Hebridean waters. Before his own submission to Bruce at the end of October 1308, the Earl of Ross wrote to Edward II as follows:

> We took the lands of the Isles from our lord the king, your father ... We assigned them to Lochlan Macruari to answer to us for their revenues. Since he refuses, may it please you, dear lord, to command him to answer to us as justice requires. For we have answered to your chamberlain for the revenues of those lands. But Lochlan is such a high and mighty lord, he'll not answer to anyone except under great force or through fear of you.
>
> Barrow, G. (1988)
> *Robert Bruce*

In other words, the Earl of Ross was financially responsible for the Northern Hebrides, but Lochlan Macruari had practical control and no intention of paying tax.

The Macruari galleys were maintained partly by levies based on the productive capacity of land. In 1304 Dugald's nephew, Lochlan, was operating against the English king, Edward I, and ordered each davach of land to furnish a galley of twenty oars. On this basis Knoydart would have supplied three galleys, each with a crew of about 22 men.

The Macruaris had their headquarters at Castle Tioram in Moidart. Although traditionally ascribed to Amy Macruari, this castle probably dates to the thirteenth century and was quite possibly a fortified site long before this. It is referred to as 'insula sicca' in a charter of Christina Macruari's dated c. 1325. This is a literal Latin translation of the Gaelic name Eilean Tioram, meaning dry or tidal island. Such a description suggests that the area was Gaelic-speaking by 1325. However, the Macruaris themselves had strong Norse contacts. Christina's cousin, Eric, travelled in Hakon of Norway's flagship in 1263 and was probably bilingual. (He has a Norse name and may have had a Norwegian mother.) In the charter, Christina granted Moidart, Arisaig, Morar, Eigg and Rum to Arthur Campbell, a supporter of Bruce. For some reason Knoydart is not included; perhaps Christina wanted to keep it for herself! In the event the whole area remained in the hands of the Macruaris.

Our earliest references to Knoydart occur in some fourteenth century charters of Robert I, David II and Robert II. These dealt with the Macruari lands before and after they passed to John of Islay by marriage. They give a variety of spellings for the district including *Knodworach, Cnudewithe, Knodworthe, Knodeworte* and *Cnudeforde*. It seems clear that the first element is the Scandinavian personal name Cnut whilst the second part is the word *fjord* or sea-loch. (It is ironic that the name Knoydart, which originally applied to Loch Nevis or Loch Hourn, now attaches to the peninsula between them. The fact that the land on the north side of the Kyles of Loch Nevis is known as Kyles Knoydart might indicate that Loch Nevis was the original Cnut's fjord but this evidence is pretty lightweight.) At any rate it is through these early references to the Macruari estates that the Norse name for the area has survived. When asked by Lowland clerks to supply lists of their territories, these Gaelic lords gave the names established by Norse colonists in previous centuries. The Viking legacy was sufficiently strong to survive a changed linguistic environment.

The Literary Evidence

There is a poem, apparently written by a Dean of Knoydart about 1490, which firmly associates Knoydart with the fortunes of Clan Donald. Ecclesiastical offices in the Middle Ages were often held by members of leading families who wished to take advantage of the church's power and wealth. The church in the Highlands was relatively impoverished but since it was endowed by the local landowners they tended to regard it as a useful source of extra revenue rather than an independent spiritual force. It was hard for the clergy to withstand temporal pressure anywhere in Europe. In the Highlands, they were cut off from external ecclesiastical support and were at the mercy of the lay authorities. Unless their lord was a particularly pious man it must have been difficult for any cleric to maintain spiritual integrity, except at monastic centres such as Iona, Oronsay, Saddell and Ardchattan.

It is in this context that we should view the benefice of Kilchoan. Pluralism, or the holding of more than one church office in order to benefit from their revenues, was the bane of religious life throughout the Middle Ages. We know that the church in Knoydart was a victim of pluralism, because by 1545 Rore Ranaldson had held the churches of Eilean Fhianain (Loch Shiel), Kilchoan (Ardnamurchan), Kilmory (Arisaig), Kilchoan (Knoydart), and was also Dean of Morvern. It is likely that he held these offices at least partly because he was brother to Clanranald, chief of one of the most important branches of Clan Donald. Fifty years earlier Knoydart was even more closely associated with Clanranald and the parsonage of Kilchoan was likely to have been in the gift of the Moidart family. This would explain the strong support for Clan Donald within the poem. It is also surprisingly un-Christian, and suggests that the author was a Macdonald propagandist first, and a churchman second.

So just who was the author? Professor Thomson has argued that it is likely to have been John Makmurich who held the parsonage of Kilchoan from 1506–1510. During the same period he also held Arisaig and Morvern. Since he held similar benefices to Rore Ranaldson, and since Morvern is in the same diocese, it may be that the title of Dean has become wrongly associated with Knoydart. His predecessor in Kilchoan was John Macdougall and after John Makmurich we learn of an Alexander Wentoun. Rore Ranaldson succeeded to Kilchoan in 1517. As a MacVurich, John was a member of a long-established literary dynasty, which helps to explain the quality of his poem.

The occasion was the punishment of Diarmaid O'Cairbre, an Irish harper who had murdered his lord, Angus Og, son and heir of John of Islay, Lord of the Isles and former Earl of Ross. Angus had fallen out with his father and defeated him at the Battle of Bloody Bay some time in the early 1480s. This was a difficult period for Clan Donald. They were coming under increasing pressure from the Scottish realm, and the Lordship had been forfeited in 1475 and then restored. Angus represented the conservative old order whilst his aged and weakened father tried to reach some sort of accommodation with the royal authorities. Angus was de facto leader of much of his clan and pursued a proud and independent course trying to restore their power – despite opposition from strong forces like the Mackenzies in the North. The Book of Clanranald, composed by successive generations of the MacVurich family, reports that:

> Angus Og had a large entertainment with the men of the
> North at Inverness, when he was murdered by Mac ICaibre,
> his own harper, who cut his throat with a long knife.

The brevity of this record may be accounted for by the fact that
one of the MacVurich family seems to have slept through the
murder whilst sharing a room with his lord. Since the
MacVurich's were hereditary bards and historians of Clanranald
they may have wanted to gloss over this inglorious episode.

Hugh Macdonald of Sleat, writing in the seventeenth
century, gives a longer account of the affair and names 'the Laird
of Knoydart' among the supporters of Angus Og. After describing
Angus's turbulent and meteoric career – which was primarily
concerned with maintaining the independence of the Lordship
against all, whether Campbell, Mackenzie or king – he provides
a detailed description of the circumstances leading to his death.
It gives a good example of the power-politics of the day, flavoured
as they were by jealousy and intrigue between dynasties and
individuals, all driven by ambition. His concluding remarks are
in some respects an epitaph on much of Highland history:

> There was another circumstance which shortened
> Macdonald's days, viz. there was a lady of the name of
> Macleod, daughter of Rory, surnamed the Black, who was
> tutor to the lawful heir of the Lewis, married to the Laird of
> Muidort. The tutor, her father, being resolved not to
> acknowledge, by any means, the true heir of the Lewis, and
> engross the whole to himself, was displaced by Macdonald,
> and the rightful heir put in possession. This lady having a
> spite at Macdonald for dispossessing her father, together with
> John Mackenzie, contrived his death in the following
> manner: There was an Irish harper of the name of Art
> O'Carby, of the county of Monaghan in Ireland, who was
> often at Macdonald's, and falling in love with Mackenzie's
> daughter, became almost mad in his amours. Mackenzie
> seeing him in that mood, promised him his daughter,
> provided he would put Macdonald to death, and made him
> swear never to reveal the secret. This fellow being afterwards
> in his cups, and playing upon his harp, used to sing the
> following verse, composed by himself in the Irish language:

'Tanmin do dhia a mharcruch neich crichd
Bhalbhrichd
Gu bheil tanmin an cansiort mata puinsuin an Gallfit'

meaning, that the rider of the dapple horse was in danger
of his life, (for Macdonald always rode such a one,) if
there was poison in his long knife, which he called Gallfit.
As Macdonald went to bed one night, there was none in
the room along with him but John Cameron, brother to
Ewan, Laird of Locheill, and Macmurrich the poet. ...
The harper rose in the night-time, when he perceived
Mac-donald was asleep, and cut his throat, for which he
was apprehended, but never confessed that he was
employed by any body so to do, although there were
several jewels found upon him, which were well known
to have belonged formerly to Mackenzie and the lady of
Muidort. The harper was drawn after horses till his limbs
were torn asunder. After the death of Angus, the Islanders,
and the rest of the Highlanders, were let loose, and began
to shed one another's blood.

Whatever the manner of his death, Diarmaid's head was exposed
as a warning to others. Angus was murdered c. 1490 and it sounds
from the content as if the author had witnessed the fate of the
murderer and wrote the poem immediately afterwards. John
Makmurich had died by July 1510 and it is just possible that he
could be 'Macmurrich the poet' referred to by Hugh Macdonald.
If it was John who slept through the murder then this may have
been his expiation. There is little historical material contained
in the poem, but it does give a notion of the spirit of the times.

THE AUTHOR OF THIS IS THE DEAN OF KNOYDART

Thou head of Diarmaid O'Cairbre, though great enough
are thy spoils and thy pride, not too great I deem the
amount of thy distress though thou hangest from a stake.

I pity not thy shaggy mane, nor (that it is tossed by) the
wind of the glens however rough; I pity thee not that a
withy is in thy jaws, thou head of Diarmaid O'Cairbre.

Woe to him who hath noted thy throat-stroke, and would not be a foe to thine alliance; woe, alas, to him who rejected not thy shrieks, thou head of Diarmaid O'Cairbre.

By thee was destroyed the king of Islay, a man who dealt wine and silver; whose locks were fresh and crisp, thou head of Diarmaid O'Cairbre.

Islay's king of festive goblets, who raised his friends to honour; woe to him who wounded his bright white skin, thou head of Diarmaid O'Cairbre.

Dear to me was his noble palm, ungrudging of gold or silver; who joyed in feast and hunting, thou head of Diarmaid O'Cairbre.

I beseech the King of the apostles, Him who protects [ ], to succour him now from pains, thou head of Diarmaid O'Cairbre.

(Watson, W. J. (ed.), 1978)

The author is aware of the barbaric nature of the punishment but adopts a vengeful and unchristian approach. He deems it worthy of the crime, states that he himself has no pity, and implies criticism of any whose resolve was shaken by the screams of the dying man. In this sense it is an affirmative poem, justifying a punishment that others might quail from. It serves a similar purpose to the *brosnachadh* or battle-incitement. It stiffened sinews and reinforced mutual loyalty.

The first three verses relish the harper's punishment, although the detail is so graphic and unpleasant as to indicate some ambivalence on the part of the poet. It is not an impersonal poem – the murderer is constantly addressed by his full name. The author's humanity was affected, even though his approach was retributive. We feel that part of the purpose of the poem is to steel himself, to reject compassion and his own Christian impulses or training. Perhaps his political position or his role as bard demanded that he adopt a firmly partisan approach. (Who is not with us is against us!) In contrast, the next three verses deal with the harper's victim, the King of Islay, whose hair was fresh and crisp, unlike Diarmaid's shaggy mane. This comparison would have meant more to contemporaries than it does to us. A great deal of attention was paid to hair in Dark Age and medieval societies. It was an important aspect of social distinction. One only has to look at the elaborate hairstyles of the kings and queens amongst the Lewis chess pieces to see how important this was in the Viking Hebrides.

The author also mourns the loss of patronage. This is a common theme amongst medieval Gaelic poets. They were, to an extent, professional and depended on the largesse of the Hebridean courts. So the King of Islay is eulogised for dispensing wine and gold and silver; for pursuing the noble art of the chase; for providing feasts and honouring his retainers. Although the sentiments are conventional, perhaps the author needed rewards from Angus to supplement a paltry income from Knoydart.

The poem is typical of a heroic, even Dark Age, approach. The only Christian sentiment in the whole work is struck in the last verse which calls on God to protect the soul of Angus from further pain – i.e. to release him from Purgatory. With this exception, the rest has sprung straight from a long pagan past.

The Sculptural Evidence

We have no architectural remains from the medieval period in Knoydart, but we do have some carved stones and a font. The absence of high-status medieval buildings is not unusual in this area of the West Highlands. We have castles at Tioram (Moidart) and Invergarry (Loch Oich), but no medieval secular buildings in Knoydart, North or South Morar, Arisaig or Moidart. The poverty of the Rough Bounds region probably meant that Clanranald and Glengarry could only afford one fortified site at Tioram and Invergarry respectively. Inverie offers no obviously defensible site and was at the periphery of the lands of either clan. There were certainly buildings here but if they were made of wood they have disappeared, and if of stone they were re-used or built over.

There are two burial grounds close to each other at Kilchoan. One of these is the site of the old church and includes two medieval grave-slabs. In the second, there is a medieval cross. Although there are other places of burial and worship in Knoydart, for instance on Eilean Tioram (Loch Nevis) and at Inverguseran, Kilchoan was always the principal religious site.

Writing in 1700, Bishop Nicolson says of Kilchoan that it is 'the burial-place of the lairds of that country'.

The cross was re-discovered by Dom Odo Blundell in the early years of this century. It is unusual in shape and design, standing apart from the run of medieval crosses (*See* Plates 4 and 5). West Highland grave-slabs and crosses follow distinctive styles between about 1350 and 1550. These have been analysed by Steer and Bannerman in their definitive volume *Late Mediaeval Monumental Sculpture in the West Highlands*. There are more than 600 grave-slabs and over sixty crosses in the series, the latter generally surviving less well, often because they were damaged or destroyed after the Reformation. The Protestant Reformers did not approve of what they thought of as idolatry, and zealously cleansed the country of offending images. Much of this destruction actually took place in the seventeenth rather than the sixteenth century and there is a trail of broken cross-heads in Islay and Kintyre as a result of the civil wars. A few West Highland crosses, such as Campbeltown, Kilchoman (Islay) and Inverary still stand, although in the case of both Campbeltown and Inverary they have been defaced by the removal of the crucifix. The cross at Kilchoan, Knoydart, is one of the handful to survive unscathed, saved by remoteness and its lack of a crucifix scene.

It is also rather idiosyncratic. It is not carved from the same stone, a greenish chlorite-schist, as most other slabs, and the shape of its head is unique. Other cross-heads, where identifiable, usually have a solid disc-head with extending rectangular arms (Campbeltown, Kilchoman, Oronsay). The Knoydart cross has expanded arms and a hole through the centre. This latter feature is reminiscent of prehistoric standing stones with perforations, such as Clach-a-Charra, Onich; the Odin Stone at Stenness in Orkney and stones at Ballymeanoch, by Kilmartin, and Kilchousland, Kintyre. The habit of using or creating perforated stones is very ancient, although we have no idea of their ritual or totemic significance in prehistoric times. All we have left are the folk traditions that survived into the Christian era. In the case of the Odin and the Argyllshire stones these included the function of sealing marriage contracts when the couple held hands through the perforation. The Odin stone also had a reputation for helping against disease. This, and the associated practice of leaving an offering such as food or cloth or stone, links it to innumerable wells and springs throughout Britain and Ireland.

We can further compare the Inverie cross with a cross slab at Camas nan Geall, Ardnamurchan. The latter was originally a prehistoric standing-stone which was absorbed into Christianity by the addition of some carved symbols between about 500 and 800 AD. On one face, the background has been cut away to leave a large Latin cross with round pellets at the armpits. Above this is a rather indistinct quadruped with a long curling tail, probably a dog. This is a good example of syncretism; where an earlier, pagan symbol has been given a Christian context. The standing-stone had marked a sacred site, which in turn became a Christian burial-ground. The dog must have been a powerful local totem since it is difficult to account for its appearance on a cross slab in any other way. In this case, a prehistoric stone has been modified to match changing religious requirements. With the Inverie cross, it is unlikely that we have a prehistoric stone which has been carved into the shape of a cross. It is more likely that we have a fifteenth century cross which has been modified by perforating the cross-head, presumably to placate local sensibilities and primeval fears. It shows that in medieval times religious observance in Knoydart was primitive and possibly downright pagan.

Here, it is relevant to quote the minutes of the Presbytery of Dingwall which met in Applecross in September 1656. The Presbytery was much exercised by bull sacrifice and 'uther abhominable and heathenishe practices' which took place on 25 August, a day dedicated to Saint Mourie (Maelrubha). The minutes record:

> that there were frequent approaches to some ruinous chappels and circulateing of them; and that future events in reference especiallie to lyfe and death, in takeing of Journeyis, was exspect to be manifested by a holl of a round stone quherein they tryed the entering of their heade, which [if they] could doe, to witt be able to put in thair heade, they exspect thair returning to that place, and failing they considered it ominous; and withall their

adoring of wells, and uther superstitious monuments and stones, tedious to rehearse.

The hole in the Inverie cross is much too small for anyone to put their head through, but it is likely that similar superstitions once prevailed in Knoydart. Like Applecross, these may have referred to the saints and sanctuaries of the early church, and beyond them to a longer pagan past. From examples elsewhere it is possible that the functions of the hole included foretelling the future, restoring health and sealing contracts. Certainly the missionary saints such as Maelrubha and Comgan brought Christianity to remote parts of the west coast, but either they or their successors were responsible for a good deal of syncretic compromise with ancestral local practice.

The face of the cross-shaft bears a single-handed sword in its lower section. The pommel and style of the sword date it to before 1500 when fashions changed and the two-handed claymore begins to appear. There is some interlace around the hole, possibly a heraldic Clanranald forearm, and a small conventional galley with furled sail at the head of the cross. The perforation made it difficult to include a crucifixion scene, which sheds light on the relative significance, in local terms, of Christ crucified, or a hole in the stone. Christian practice in Knoydart was certainly idiosyncratic.

The reverse of the cross-head shows a mounted horseman, which is a frequent motif, but the back of the main shaft is remarkable because it seems to portray Daniel in the lions' den. This is a common Early Christian motif but I am not otherwise aware of it in a medieval context in the West Highlands. The scene is set sideways down the shaft and is difficult to interpret because it is so badly worn. A small figure, largely head, ears and eyes, is inverted between two quadrupeds, which I take to be lions. Why this motif should occur in Knoydart is an enigma. It is always possible that there is a now lost Early Christian stone in the neighbourhood from which the sculptor drew his theme.

There are also two mediaeval grave-slabs which are more typical of the West Highland series. One stone can be dated to the sixteenth rather than fifteenth century because it includes a claymore or two-handed sword. This is thought to have come into fashion c. 1500 and predominated for about a century. The head of the stone is triangular, which is unusual. At the foot of the slab are two common motifs, a hunting-scene and a galley under sail, but what makes this slab remarkable is the presence of an archer.

In all the 700 or so stones in the West Highland series, only four show bows and arrows. This is despite the fact that we know that archery was popular here and survived longer than elsewhere in Britain. One example is on a panel of a wall-tomb at Rodel, Harris; the other two are in Arisaig. The proximity of Kilmory, (Arisaig), to Kilchoan, (Knoydart), and the fact that they were both held from 1517 by Rore Ranaldson, brother of Clanranald, suggest these stones are part of a group. Rore's own grave-slab occurs at the priory of Ardchattan where there is a cross carved by John O'Brolchan in 1500. The O'Brolchans were a family famous for masons and clerics, and it is quite possible that a master-mason from Ardchattan was employed for a while at Kilmory and Kilchoan. After the collapse of the Lordship of the Isles, the earlier schools of sculpture at Saddell, Iona and Oronsay were partially replaced by small workshops surviving under local patronage. One or two craftsmen may have flourished for a time in Arisaig under John of Moidart's protection. In addition to the link with Kilchoan through his brother Rore, one of John's wives was daughter of the Laird of Knoydart.

The second slab shows some fairly coarse interlaced foliage and at the foot is a pair of shears. This is a common enough motif in certain areas, particularly in grave-slabs from Kintyre, but is a little unexpected in Knoydart. It is unlikely that it was a purely conventional symbol and suggests that wool was a significant local commodity. Although we associate Knoydart with a cattle economy in the eighteenth century perhaps sheep were important before, as they were again afterwards.

The cross, the grave-slabs, the church (of which only the font survives), all indicate a family of some consequence. Can we attribute any of the stones to one particular individual? On the evidence of the sword-design, the cross is likely to be fifteenth century, perhaps associated with the founder of the Knoydart family, Allan, or either of his successors John or Ranald. Allan may have wished to mark the founding of his house with some symbolic act such as setting up an imposing cross in the local churchyard. The grave-slab with the claymore may belong to Angus McAllan McRanald who was a supporter of Donald Dubh's rising in 1545. He would have known Rore Ranaldson well and was a stalwart Clanranald activist.

Bishop Nicolson, who visited the area in 1700, reported the belief that these carved stones came from Iona – a common presumption, but one which we can discount. These are local products, with local idiosyncrasies – which makes them all the more interesting. All three stones in Kilchoan are a little unsophisticated in design and a little inexpert in execution. This is perfectly comprehensible. They represent attempts by the local ruling family to match a wealth and an expertise they could see in ideal form in the richer centres of Iona, Oronsay or Kintyre. They represent Knoydart's share of a common West Highland culture.

Chapter 5

KNOYDART IN THE LATER MIDDLE AGES

Constructing a history for Knoydart between the fifteenth and seventeenth centuries faces serious problems. First there is a paucity of documents. Where we do come across the names of individuals from Knoydart amongst the official records they are usually in the form – A, son of B, son of C. Surnames were not yet fixed and the possibilities for confusion are endless. It is difficult enough to construct an agreed genealogy for the early lairds of Knoydart, let alone any other family.

Further problems arise from the very nature of history-making in the Highlands. Traditionally, a great deal of Highland history has been *family* history. This is both a strength and a weakness. It is a strength because unless families had passed down their traditions from one generation to the next, much of the early history of the Highlands would be unknown. It is a weakness because family historians are notoriously liable to omit or distort historical facts that are prejudicial to their own line. Historians from other families may give a different version, or none at all. Where official records exist they are usually written from a Lowland perspective and are either unsympathetic to, or ignorant of, a Highland viewpoint.

These weaknesses are particularly apparent in the context of Knoydart. The clan historians have given us some early family history while the official records add the names of a few individuals, usually because they were in trouble with the authorities. For some of the 'facts' we have nothing more than the strength of tradition, and not all of the pieces of evidence are in agreement

with each other. Different historians have promoted or relegated different 'facts' in support of their own case. For example, at the beginning of the nineteenth century there was a ferocious argument over precedence between the champions of the Glengarry and Clanranald families. Knoydart was invoked in the sense that it became an issue as to which family the area had originally belonged to. From a present perspective the whole controversy seems extraordinary and misguided. What follows accords with the Clanranald line of argument rather than the Glengarry, but it must be admitted that the thread of evidence is very slender.

Most Macdonald historians have taken the view that the original lairds of Knoydart were an offshoot of the Clanranald family. They trace descent from Allan (second chief of Clanranald) whose second son, Allan, was the first of Knoydart. Hence the line was known as *Sliochd Ailein Mhic Ailein* (the Seed of Allan, son of Allan). Ranald, last of the line, was supposedly killed at Rubha Raonuill near Glaschoille about 1613. The evidence for this early Knoydart line is sparse. Some of them appear in the public records, others do not, and their dates are speculative (*See* Figure 3).

We can add to this family tree with evidence from elsewhere. Hugh Macdonald of Sleat, one of our earliest family sources, wrote his history of the Macdonalds during the seventeenth century. This was the same century as the Glengarry takeover, a political event of considerable local importance and one of which he showed himself aware. On two separate occasions he specifically states that the Knoydart family was an offshoot of the Macdonalds of Clanranald. His account, as printed in *Collectanea de Rebus Albanicis* (1847) refers to 'Allan, son to Allan, Laird of Muidart, of whom descended the ancient family of Knoydart'. Further on, when writing of Alexander of Glengarry, he says 'At that time the lands of Knoidart did not belong to him, for they were possessed by a younger branch of the family of Muidort'. MacVurich, the other early historian of the Macdonalds, also refers to an independent Laird of Knoydart in a sixteenth century context. Timothy Pont, who cannot be accused of any family bias, referred to a local Laird of Knoydart when he made his notes on the area, probably in the 1590s.

Knoydart is not mentioned in official documents as part of Glengarry's estate during the sixteenth century. In a roll of Highland landlords appended to an Act of Parliament of 1587 the 'Larde of Glengarry' and the 'Laird of Knoydert' are listed separately. This negative evidence, and what we know of the transfer of ownership between 1611 and 1613, confirms that Knoydart was not originally possessed by Glengarry. It belonged to a younger branch of the Moidart family. This branch became increasingly independent of the parent clan before succumbing to their distant cousins, the Glengarry family, early in the seventeenth century. However, there remains the problem of why North Morar, located just south of Knoydart, should have passed to Glengarry at a much earlier date. The common heritage of these territories is confirmed by the fact that Acts of Parliament in 1587 and 1594, dealing with 'brokin men' in the Highlands, both refer to the *Clanranald* of Knoydart, Moidart and Glengarry. These lands were part of the old Macruari patrimony.

From Clanranald to Glengarry

Knoydart belonged to different branches of the same family for at least 700 years. This made for an extraordinary continuity since many local families enjoyed uninterrupted possession from about 1150. There was some disruption in 1613, not all of it peaceful, as the Glengarry family established themselves. The old lairds sank into oblivion whilst the new family moved into positions of dominance. One of their first acts, in 1614, was to give a wadset of Inverguseran to Alexander Oig, who was one of the old order and their bitter opponent just a year before. (A wadset was a loan, in this case to the chief, which allowed the lender the use and profits of the land whilst the loan remained outstanding.) However, Glengarry's own people gradually assumed the reins of power. Almost all the later landholders in Knoydart trace their origin to the chief's line. Younger sons founded cadet families; principally of Scottos, (from which the main line was twice revitalised) and Barrisdale. The house of Scottos in turn founded dynasties in Sandaig (Lochgarry), Crowlin and Ardnaslishnish. By the time of the 1745 Rising, Knoydart was as completely controlled by Glengarry as it had once been by Clanranald.

For the ordinary people of Knoydart the change in ownership made little or no difference to their daily lives. Their political orientation shifted east to the Glengarry base at Invergarry by Loch Oich. This merely involved them in a different set of quarrels and possibly an increased level of land traffic. There remains the problem of just how the Glengarry family managed to wrest Knoydart from another major branch of Clan Donald. We have only the barest facts to guide us.

In 1537, James V gave the lands of Knoydart to Donald Cameron of Lochiel. The relevant charter claims that Knoydart had been in the King's hands for the previous 70 years since the death of the last lawful owner. We should not take this too literally. The king did not control Knoydart, it simply meant that the Knoydart chiefs had declined to pay their feudal entry dues to the Scottish realm since 1467. Accordingly, James regarded their lands as technically his to dispose of. In practice, cession to Donald Cameron made little difference on the ground. The Camerons did not own Knoydart in anything more than a legal sense, although the charter became important in 1611 when Lochiel transferred ownership to the Macdonells of Glengarry. There may have been significant Cameron involvement in Knoydart during the sixteenth century, probably as a result of intermarriage. Certainly their lands marched together and would have seen some commercial and personal traffic. However, the Clanranald family was then a powerful entity, particularly during the long reign of John Moydartach, and Knoydart would not be disposed of except with his consent.

By the beginning of the seventeenth century circumstances were different. In 1602, the Laird of Knoydart is mentioned as one of Glengarry's henchmen in the context of a raid on Torridon. Again the most likely reason for such a political and military association is by intermarriage. In 1611, Lochiel transferred ownership to Glengarry and, in 1613, the King confirmed this. For Lochiel the legal possession of Knoydart was probably no more than a useful bargaining counter. He stood to gain little from it, except as a lever to extract benefits from Glengarry. He probably came to a political decision that Knoydart was incapable of being subdued, or not worth it, or both. What then were the precise circumstances of the change in ownership?

It appears from subsequent events that not all the principal tenants in Knoydart were inclined to accept the new Glengarry overlordship. In 1613 they murdered a certain Ronald MacAngus Gear (? *geàrr* = short) in Neogart and then compounded their offence by raiding the lands of Laggan Achadrom in Glengarry, where they fired some houses. The mention of the murdered man in the same context as the raid suggests that the victim may have been some sort of local representative or adherent of Glengarry's, possibly a relation of the chief. Glengarry appealed to higher authority and commissions were granted to himself, Mackenzie of Coigach, Macleod of Dunvegan and Grant of Freuchie to proceed against the men of Knoydart. This commission is interesting because it gives us the names of some of the tenants in Kilchoan, Sandaig, Inverguseran, Ardnaslishnish and Crowlin.

> Commission ... to apprehend and present to justice Allan McAllaster VcAngus in Kilchoan ... Donald McAngus McAllan in Sandok ... Alexander Oig in Innergizeran, Ronald Roy in Ardinsletherache, Angus McAllane Roy in Crobling

According to tradition, Ranald, the last chief of the Knoydart line, was put to death by Glengarry's men at Rudha Raonuill (Ranald's point) near Glaschoille about 1613. In 1614, Glengarry gave a wadset of 5d of Inverguseran to Alexander Oig, who was one of the raiders in 1613. By this means local opposition was squared and Knoydart came under Glengarry's control. However, this was not quite the end of the matter. Some elements of Clanranald were reluctant to let this important district pass completely to another clan, albeit a related one, and subsequently mounted heavy raids on Knoydart.

The question is why did Clanranald permit property, that had originally been part of his clan's territory, go to the family of Glengarry? There are a number of possible answers. Knoydart had belonged to a separate branch of the clan from as early as the 1420s. Perhaps the Knoydart family had been pursuing such an independent course as to warrant little sympathy or help from the parent branch of Clanranald. Glengarry's estate of North Morar separated Clanranald's lands in Moidart and Arisaig from Knoydart, so this may also have been a factor in his decision to relinquish any claim. Finally, the family of Clanranald was suffering from considerable turmoil at the time. The chief had limited control over some of his unruly relations and the lack of internal unity resulted in a degree of political weakness.

The two branches of Clan Donald eventually came to terms in a document whose cryptic language disguises a violent usurpation which Clanranald was constrained to accept. It is difficult to explain such territorial loss unless in terms of his domestic difficulties and Glengarry's ability to exploit the situation. Glengarry certainly enjoyed political support from Edinburgh and other Highland chiefs.

On 18 July 1616 a contract was drawn up between Donald MacAllan MacIain of Castle Tioram (Clanranald) and Donald MacAngus (Glengarry). This agreement was designed to patch up the quarrels between the two chieftains, particularly over Knoydart, and may well have been the result of royal pressure. Under its terms:

> Donald M'Allane V'Eane of Ilandterim … faithfullie binds and obleiss him and his airis that he his men tennentis and servandis … sall in na tyme cuming harme skaithe trubill molest nor oppres the said Donald M'Angus of Glengarie and his airis thair men tennentis & servandis kyn nor frinds in thair bodyes landis or guidis under ye paine of four thousand punds.

Since taking such blanket responsibility for all his wayward clansmen was more than Clanranald could readily agree to, his lawyers secured him something like an insurance excess clause

> provyding allwayes that ye said skaithe damage and interes to be sustenit be ye said laird of Glengarie and his forsaids extend the soume of thrie scoir punds.

In other words, he would not be responsible for the first £60 of loss. It further appears that Glengarry's tenants had something of a claim against Clanranald's men for a raid in May:

> it is pretendit be ye said laird of Glengarie that in ye month of May last bypast Johne and Rorie M'Allane VcEane committit ane heirschip in ye said laird of Glengarie's land of Knoydert be taking away of certane guidis furt of ye said cuntrie of Knoydert.

Clanranald promises to restore the goods taken

> … be ye saids Johne and Rorie McAllanes VcEanes and thair complices.

provided that:

> ye samen be first provin and verefeit be Alester McEane VcAllane in Innerzeistherim, Angus McAllane Roy in Lie, Alester his broyer in Crolin, & Neill McRorie VcEan Roy in Scottos.

Although Glengarry bound himself in the same terms, it sounds as if he was the plaintiff. It appears that some of the Clanranald had mounted a large scale raid on the coastal strip between Scottos and Li during May. It is likely that this was just the last and most serious of a long series of raids and reprisals, since each chief promises compensation to the other for damages sustained before 27 February 1615. Glengarry's claim is partially offset by what is effectively a counterclaim by Clanranald's lawyers for past damages sustained at the hands of

> ye said Donald McAngus and his forsaids and namelie be Alaster McEan VcAllane Roy in Lie, Alaster his broyer, Allane Moir in Barristel and Ronnald Roy McEan VcAllane in Ardnasteisneithe.

Here we probably have one of the victims himself accused of having raided Clanranald's lands previously, along with accomplices from Li, Barrisdale and Ardnaslishnish. It is impossible to do more than guess at the true course of events. There may have been raiding and counter-raiding between Knoydart and Arisaig for years. Certainly neither set of lawyers would let their clients accept sole responsibility. At any rate, matters were now to be settled. Clanranald gave an assurance that he would no longer succour Glengarry's opponents in Knoydart:

> the said Donald McAllane VcEane binds and obleiss him and his forsaids to concure fortifie and assist the said Donald McAngus and his airis againes all his maties rebellis of Knoydert that molestis and troubillis the cuntrie.

In return, Glengarry agreed to drop any actions against Clanranald

And finally Donald McAngus discharges all uyer actiones
that he may haif againes the said Donald McAllane VcEane.

Glengarry was the winner in all this. Essentially, Clanranald
gave up any further claim on Knoydart.

After the turmoil of 1611–1616 the internal political history
of Knoydart at last settled down. However, within a broader
Scottish framework, the seventeenth century was a troubled
period. There were the Montrose Wars of the 1640s and the
conflicts surrounding the accession of William and Mary. Some
of Knoydart's inhabitants would have been caught up in these
campaigns. They had always had to be soldiers of fortune for
reasons of economic necessity. Now they were fighting for greater
causes which their leaders signed them up to.

Even outside these conflicts Knoydart folk proved
troublesome for the authorities. We find their names recurring
in official documents, but seldom do we have more detail than a
name, or a string of patronymics, followed by a place of residence.
In 1628, Thomas Fraser of Strichen led a legal action pursuing
Donald Gorme McVcAlaster in Berrisdaill (and thirty-three
others) for theft. In the same year, a commission was granted to
apprehend Martine McEane VcRorie VcEane Roy in Knoydart
(among others) for theft and arson. In 1666, a number of
Macdonalds including Ronald McDonald in Ley, Angus McDonald
in Crolig, and Donald McEachin in Knoydart were involved in
a bloody fracas in Inverness although, of course, they were
'conscious of their oune innocency'.

That they were not always innocent is suggested by an entry in
the Privy Council records in July 1602. A large party of Glengarry's
men, including the 'Laird of Knodort' and 'Donnald McAngus
Geir', had been involved in a bloody raid on Torridon which left at
least seven men dead. Donald McAngus Gair may be the same as
the Ronald who was murdered in 1613 but it seems as if the men
of Knoydart, whilst still independent in 1602, were then supporters
and friends of Glengarry. In November 1601 Glengarry's men, along
with a great number of 'brokin and disorderit Hielandmen', all
armed with pole-axes, claymores, 'hagbuts and pistolets' came, by
night, to their victims' houses in Torridon. What follows could
come straight from an Icelandic saga:

and thair the saidis disorderit personis awfullie and tressonablie set fyre about the saidis houssis and had almaist cruellie and unmercifullie brunt thame thairin, wer not thay, for eschewing of the furie of the fyre, comeing furth of the saidis housses upoun esperance and houp that mercy sould have bene schawne to thame, [after which the said persons] spairit thame a little space, [but at last] maist cruellie, schamefullie and mercyleslie murtherit and slew [them all] and kaist thame in the fyre.

That Knoydart was effectively independent of central authority is proven by a plea of 1669 from the sheriff-clerk of Inverness. George Leslie asked to be excused from the task of uplifting the King's taxes in:

Knoydart, Moydart, Glengarie and other hieland parts, whose inhabitants are not legallie disposed nor willing to his Majesties dues, being infested with poverty and idlnes … seing disobedience hes bein given be them to the pairties of his Majesties forces of a considerable strenth.

Happily, the Lords of the Privy Council had some sympathy with him and excused him his task.

For the seventeenth century, and particularly the first half of the eighteenth, the people of Knoydart had a dreadful reputation. They were renowned for thieving and, although this was carried on with great success by Coll of Barrisdale, there would eventually be a day of reckoning. Within a century of George Leslie's plea the Barrisdale estate was being run directly by government.

Religion

Religious affiliation in the Highlands after the Reformation was very much a matter for the clan chief. The area of the Rough Bounds remained staunchly Catholic and as a result earned any amount of abuse from eighteenth century Protestant writers. In general terms, ignorance, thieving and political disaffection were inextricably linked to Catholicism. Knoydart was, according to the Presbytery of Gairloch in 1763, 'the most unmixed nest of Popery in all the Highlands' and required 'that a particular regard be had to the manner of reforming and civilising it'.

Almost as a reaction, the Rough Bounds have been viewed favourably by Catholic historians as a last refuge of native Catholicism. They defend the area with pride and recount the traditional Catholic associations. Both of these viewpoints are of limited relevance. Catholicism could hardly be equated with thieving and disaffection when the Protestant Camerons were also such staunch Jacobites and cattle-reivers. Alexander Macbean, Minister of Inverness, wrote in 1746:

> The Camerons boast of their being Protestants, and Lochiel hindered his brother the priest to preach among them, when he told him he would bring them from that villainous habit of thieving, if he would allow him to preach, and say Mass among them: his answer was that the people of Glengarry, Knoidart, Arisag, etc., who were profest Papists, were greater thieves than his people, and if he would bring these to be honest and industrious, he would then consider his proposal as to the Camerons, and till he would bring that good work to a bearing he positively forbad him to meddle with his people.

However, some contemporary commentators give the impression that in parts of the West Highlands there was not much of any religion. Perhaps the situation was as described by Bruce in 1750 when talking of Colin McKenzie, 1st Earl of Seaforth. He writes:

> He planted Ministers among them who by his Influence brought the People rather from Heathenish Darkness than Popery.

Chapter 6

THE JACOBITES IN KNOYDART

There is an explosion of documentary evidence for Knoydart in the eighteenth century. For most of its previous history we have only scraps with which to conjure. From now on we are on firmer ground.

The evidence is of several types and of differing value. We have topographical reports supplied by travellers; we have chance comments by contemporary letter writers like Mrs Grant of Laggan; we have biographical sketches of some of Knoydart's prominent individuals, Coll Barrisdale, Macdonald of Scottos, Raonull Mor a' Chrolen and Spanish John. We have references in documents concerned with the Jacobite Risings; we have poetry by Alasdair Macdonald and, above all, we have the Forfeited Estates Papers. This last presents us with such a substantial body of evidence that it will be dealt with in a separate chapter.

Knoydart now belonged to the family of Glengarry and took part in their adventures. Although Glengarry was the clan chief in 1745, a large proportion of Knoydart was actually wadset to Barrisdale and Scottos. Both these families were cadets of Glengarry and shared their chief's background and outlook. The consequences of their political orientation proved disastrous for the common people of Knoydart.

In the first half of the eighteenth century the exiled Stuart family made three attempts to regain the British throne – in 1714, 1719 and 1745–6. All ended in failure. The people of Knoydart, courtesy of their landlords, were heavily involved in the

Risings, particularly the last, and suffered the consequences of defeat. In 1755 the estate of Barrisdale was forfeited and until 1784 it was run by the Commissioners for the Forfeited Estates.

There is an enormous, and growing, body of historical work to do with the Jacobites. Unfortunately far too much of this is romantic claptrap. Some authors are less interested in the harsh facts than in playing on our sympathy for the underdog and the undoubted attraction of the tale. Looked at objectively, the Jacobite Risings in general, and 1745 in particular, were a disastrous political diversion for Highlanders. It condemned them to the role of unwilling, backward and reactionary participants in the new Britain that was being forged in the eighteenth century. It was not until much later in the same century that any attention was given to their endemic problems and, although there has been plenty of sympathy since, there have been no solutions. The best epitaph on Bonnie Prince Charlie's adventure was given by John Macdonald of Borrodale, an active participant. Of the prince's departure he said that he 'left us all in a worse state than he found us'.

I do not intend to review the Risings except in so far as they touch on Knoydart. However, the consequences of failure in 1746 were severe, lasting and had immediate effect. Glengarry's men were raised under his second son, Angus, who was accidentally killed in Falkirk in 1746. Subordinate commands were held by Macdonell of Lochgarry (originally the house of Sandaig), Coll of Barrisdale, Donald Macdonell of Scottos, John Macdonell of Crowlin and other members of the Barrisdale and Scottos families. What this meant for the ordinary people of Knoydart was that they were called up by their landowners who were all cadets of Glengarry's family. Service was not a voluntary matter. Contemporary letters from recruiting agents like Coll Macdonald of Barrisdale are full of threats as to what would happen to the homes and possessions of those men who did not respond to their summons.

In Moidart there is evidence that not all the common people viewed the Rising with the same fervour as their landowners or propagandists like the poet Alexander Macdonald. Time of course proved them right – when they suffered for the rashness and folly of their superiors. After Culloden, the people of the Rough Bounds displayed resentment against those who had called down the wrath of government. Bruce found

> The People of these Wild Countries could never believe
> that they were Accessible 'till the King's Forces Scoured
> them after the Battle of Culloden which was a prodigious
> Surprize to the Inhabitants. The Common people, tho'
> Papists, Curse their Prince and Chiefs together, as they
> are sensible that all their Calamities are owing to them.

If they had succeeded, of course, things would have been
different. But in the cold light of day Bonnie Prince Charlie
appeared no more than an adventurer, a political opportunist,
whose failure cost many others their lives and possessions. He
was fully warned of the resources he needed to bring if the Rising
was to have any chance of success. He did not; it failed; and
many Highland lives were ruined.

The men from Knoydart were assembled in two contingents,
those brought by Coll Macdonald of Barrisdale and those under
Donald Macdonald of Scottos. Lochgarry tells us that, a week after
the standard was raised at Glenfinnan, the Prince was at Invergarry
to pick up the Glengarry men.

> That same day young Scotus and young and old Barrisdales
> arrived at Auchendroom [Achadrom] with your Cnoidart
> and Morar men, who made a very handsom appearance
> before the Prince, being compleatly armed, and most of them
> had targes.

It is unlikely that there were many, if any, casualties in Coll's troop.
The Battle of Prestonpans was over in a few minutes and they
took no part in Culloden, being several miles away when it was
fought. Scottos fared differently. He was killed at Culloden along
with at least twenty-two of his fifty men. Most of these were
probably from the Scottos estate, which consisted of the lands
round Scottos itself and farms facing Loch Nevis. Culloden
therefore had immediate consequences for Knoydart. A number
of the young men were killed, which must have caused considerable
hardship and heartache in the farms from which they came. Others
suffered transportation. John McDonald of Glengarry's regiment
was transported on 31 March 1747 and is described as being a
'Labourer on the land of the Laird of Scotus'.

Worse still, a punishment expedition visited Knoydart in 1746 and carried off the cattle. The *Memorial for John Macdonald of Glengarry* (*1750*) describes how Glengarry was forced to accompany one of Cumberland's punishment parties:

> from whence they proceeded and the Memorialist along with them to Knoidart, all the cattle of which country that party drove away after they surrendered and sometime after that burned and destroyed it in the same manner as Glengarry had been.

We have an anonymous contemporary account of the huge quantities of livestock sold off cheaply by Fort Augustus.

> Whilst our Army stayed here, we had near twenty Thousand Head of Cattle brought in, such as Oxen, Horses, Sheep, and Goats, taken from the Rebels (whose Houses we also frequently plundered and burnt) by Parties sent out for them, and in Search of the Pretender; so that great Numbers of our Men grew rich by their Shares in the Spoil, which was bought up, by the Lump, by Jockeys and Farmers, from Yorkshire, and the South of Scotland; and the Money was divided amongst the Men, and few Common Soldiers were without Horses.

Similarly, when Coll Barrisdale returned to Knoydart, he found the cattle gone:

> the army had eaten up one part of them, and some of the clergy hastening to be rich, bought the other. Rose, the minister of Nairn ... purchased a number of them at five shillings per head, tho' he did not increase his store by his bargain, for many of them died thro' the change of grass, and other inconveniences.

To the beneficiaries this must have seemed a just retribution on the notorious thieves of Knoydart, at whose hands they had so often suffered before Culloden. To the people of the Jacobite clans it would have been an economic disaster. Cattle were their livelihood. They stole because they had to, and although we have no records to tell us, there must have been considerable misery and hunger in the winter of 1746–7 and for several years after. This was war, eighteenth-century style, and it was unpleasant. By contrast with later times, such as during the Clearances or the potato famine, there was little sympathy for the Highlanders in their predicament. Simple retribution was favoured then and there is no doubt that many from other parts of Scotland had suffered at Highland hands. On the retreat from Derby a robbery took place in Dumfries in which two of Macdonald of Scottos's men were implicated. Some of the stolen goods were found on their persons and returned. Scottos behaved honourably but no doubt the incident served to reinforce a stereotype of the Highlanders which worked to their disadvantage until Jacobitism and cattle-raids were only a memory.

With all the euphemisms adopted when talking of the Jacobite Risings, we are inclined to forget that this was essentially a civil war, arguably the most unpleasant and traumatic of all types of war because the cohesion of the social group is torn apart. Even within the West Highlands and Islands not all the clans took up arms for Charles, whilst other Highlanders opposed him. Macdonald of Scottos had a son fighting for the Hanoverians and he was terrified by the thought that he might unwittingly kill his own child. In the event, the son was taken prisoner by the father, but his situation was horrendous.

In order to explore the effect of the 1745 Rising on Knoydart and its people we shall look at it through biographical sketches of some of its participants. This period is the first in which we have real characters to sketch. Before this we have only had the names of people, places or events. Now we have flesh-and-blood, warts-and-all individuals to deal with. Unfortunately, we sometimes only have one source for these cameos which means they are biased, but this is still preferable to nothing at all. We will glimpse the history of Knoydart through the persons of Coll Macdonald of Barrisdale, as described by several; Macdonald of Scottos, by the Chevalier de Johnstone; Spanish John, as retold by himself; and Raonull Mor a' Chrolen, as sketched by Fraser-Mackintosh and Charles Macdonald.

Such an approach gives a flavour of contemporary events, but unfortunately it is restricted to the concerns of great men and particular families. The justification is that they alone held political and economic power in a society that was still extra-ordinarily hierarchical.

Coll Macdonald of Barrisdale

The character of Coll Macdonald returns us to the problem of historiography already touched on in an earlier chapter. A great deal of Highland history has been written by family historians who adopt a political rather than a strictly historical approach to their subject. They view it as incumbent upon themselves to defend the honour and integrity of their, or their adopted, family against the slurs and insinuations of detractors from other less worthy, noble or high-born tribes. This clannish amour propre bedevilled Highland history-making in the nineteenth century. What is more, since these same nineteenth-century historians produced classic volumes which, for size and erudition, are unlikely to be repeated, it bedevils us yet. Nowhere is this better seen than in the portraits of Coll Macdonald of Barrisdale.

In outlining the character of Coll, the clan historians tell us of his classical education, his handsome figure, his commanding presence etc. No doubt these are all true but there other *contemporary* reports which suggest that he was little more than a sadistic thug who ran a very successful protection racket. To arrive at a closer view of the matter, let us look at some of these accounts.

Perhaps the most revealing occurs in an anonymous description of the Highlands written in 1750. The author of this was probably a Mr Bruce who was employed by Glengarry before and after the Jacobite Rising. He certainly acted as a Government agent and though he had little sympathy for the chiefs he was not without feeling for their clansmen. Being Protestant and Whig, he viewed the conservative Catholic chiefs with suspicion and some of his arguments appear surprisingly modern and democratic. Mr Bruce's manuscript was edited by Andrew Lang, an author much vilified by Clan Donald historians for his contention that Alasdair Ruadh, chief of Glengarry, was none other than Pickle the Spy, a notorious government informer. Bruce's manuscript takes the form of a descriptive tour. He starts in the Northern Highlands, travels west to the Hebrides and then returns to the Rough Bounds of the west coast.

In all the Countries I have yet travel'd through the People

Plate 1: Knoydart from space. *(CNES/DERA)*

Plate 2: Knoydart in Blaeu. *(Trustees of the National Library of Scotland)*

Plate 3a and 3b: Early Christian cross-slab, Kilchoan. *(D. Rixson)*

Plate 4: Medieval cross, Kilchoan. *(D. Rixson)*

Plate 5b: Sword on medieval cross, Kilchoan. *(D. Rixson)*

Plate 5a: Daniel? *(D. Rixson)*

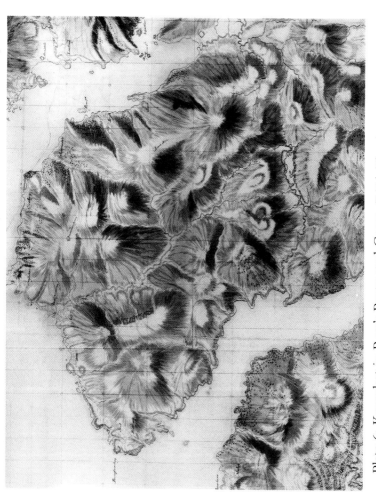

Plate 6: Knoydart in Roy's Protracted Copy. *(British Library)*

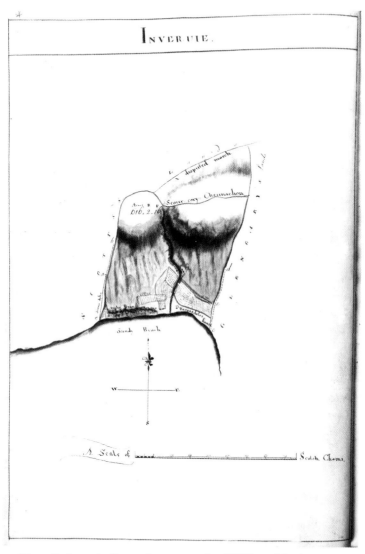

Plate 7: Inverie farm-plan, 1771, by William Morison.
(By permission of the Keeper of the Records of Scotland – (E741/47 f 10v)

Plate 8: Daniell: The Bay of Barrisdale in Loch Hourne. *(Trustees of the National Library of Scotland)* 'During the herring season this sequestered loch becomes the busy resort of numerous vessels employed in this productive fishery. It was at such a period, with the favourable accompaniment of a fresh breeze, while they were working in every direction, that the present view was taken.' *(A Voyage round Great Britain (1819))*

Live by their own Labour and Industry and are no more given to Theft than the Lowland Countries, but as I proceeded on the Coast Southward I came to Knoidart which is a perfect Den of Thieves and Robbers ... The Inhabitants of this Country have been ever Wild Rapacious and a plague and Disturbance to their Neighbours, but they have within these few years exceeded their ordinary Bounds.

Bruce describes how Coll of Barrisdale entered into an alliance with Macdonald of Lochgarry, Clan Cameron and some ruffians from Rannoch. Between them, these chieftains ran an armed band which they used to terrorise the neighbouring clans to the north, east and south. When the thieves took a spoil their chiefs subtracted a proportion for themselves. Over a period of time the neighbouring clans wearied of these incessant raids and organized themselves to maintain armed men for self-protection. Barrisdale realised that this would end his lucrative enterprise and so arranged to protect the victims himself, in return for a substantial financial consideration. Put into modern terms this was a protection racket, with Barrisdale taking the proceeds and letting his men loose in the event of non-compliance. It was said that in 1743 he had '180 Targets ... ready for use' (Targets = soldiers, because they carried targes or shields).

Historians with a strong loyalty to a particular clan or family tend to put a positive spin on such allegations. Of the same incident the Clan Donald historians said, in 1904:

About this time [i.e. the 1730s and 1740s] he was made Captain of the Watch and Guardian of the Marches on the west side of Inverness-shire, a position to which he was appointed by the neighbouring proprietors who had combined to protect themselves from the cattle-raiding which was so common at the time. Barrisdale ... did more than any other to put an end to the demoralising custom of cattle-lifting.

Both of these views cannot be correct and there is no doubt that the reverend brothers A and A Macdonald were being more than a little disingenuous! Bruce was undoubtedly prejudiced,

but he was not necessarily unfair. He goes on to say that he
'could not find' that the Macdonalds of Scottos 'were in the
least concerned with Thieving'. Bruce's account of Coll's
activities is confirmed by Murray of Broughton and the
anonymous author of the *Life of Barisdale* written in 1754.
Referring to those who dealt in black cattle the latter says:

> in a meeting among themselves at Redcastle ... they
> proposed to Barisdale a praemium from each, in
> proportion to the number of cows he had, in order to be
> protected in their property; the terms were accepted, and
> the reward was to be paid in meal, a commodity not much
> abounding in the highlands; and as it was to be given for
> preservation of the black cattle, so the name of black meal
> was given it.
>
> Barisdale, having got his commission, played his cards
> with both hands. No man appear'd more terrible against
> thieves, when in the midst of his constituents, and no
> man more mild than he, when in the midst of his gang;
> over whom he exercised as rigorous an authority, as the
> most absolute monarch can be supposed to do.

On the other hand, it could be argued that Barrisdale was
behaving like a responsible patriarch in providing a solution to
a problem of overpopulation in Knoydart. As we shall see in
the next chapter it may be that Knoydart's population had
expanded beyond what the land could normally sustain as early
as the 1730s. It is significant that Barrisdale secured a payment
in kind rather than coin. Black meal, of course, would have
been a staple for the inhabitants of his Knoydart estate.

Making moral judgements on Barrisdale's conduct is
complicated and irrelevant. He could be cast as a chieftain in
the heroic mould, saving his numerous clansmen from starvation
by means of the traditional *creach* or raid. Or he could be viewed
as a godfather figure who tolerated the misdeeds of others
provided it suited him. Certainly he drew immense profits from
his forays. Not only did he build a magnificent mansion at Inverie
but he also lent a great deal of money to Glengarry, who gave
him the wadsets of a large part of Knoydart in return. As Andrew
Fletcher wrote in 1746 'Barisdale could sell Glengary in a

mercat'. He certainly passed into Highland mythology as a larger-than-life figure. Pennant in his *Voyage to the Hebrides*, written later in the century, writes of

> the celebrated Barrisdale, who carried these arts [of stealing] to the highest pitch of perfection: besides exerting all the common practices, he improved that article of commerce called the black-meal to a degree beyond what was ever known to his predecessors. This was a forced levy, so called from its being commonly paid in meal, which was raised far and wide on the estate of every nobleman and gentleman, in order that their cattle might be secured from the lesser thieves, over whom he secretly presided, and protected. He raised an income of five hundred a year by these taxes: and behaved with genuine honor in restoring, on proper consideration, the stolen cattle of his friends. ... [Whilst] observing a strict fidelity towards his own gang; yet he was indefatigable in bringing to justice any rogues that interfered with his own.

It also says something about Barrisdale's character that he earned quite a reputation for himself amongst his contemporaries as the inventor of a peculiar instrument of torture. It may not have been so terrible in practice as it was by repute, but there were not many of his time or place who went so far to ensure obedience. The *Life of Barisdale* gives some details:

> He had machines for putting them to different sorts of punishments; such as went away without acquainting his comrade, was put into the stocks, which lay before his own door at the head of a bay that gives him his title, and as a mortification to the criminal, his back was set to the sea, and his face to the house, where victuals were brought before him, but he prohibted to eat under the severest penalties; nor did he get any food to sustain him for twenty-four hours, except bread and water. The people guilty of a fouler offence, such as not giving him a share of the cows that had been stolen, was bound with cords

and thrown into a dungeon, while those who were suspected of having seized a booty and not acknowledging it, were put to the torture, and a confession extorted from them in the following manner:

The supposed criminal was tied to an iron machine, where a ring grasped his feet, and another closed upon his neck, and his hands were received into eyes of iron contrived for the purpose; to move his hands or feet was impracticable, tho' his neck was at a little more liberty, but then he had a great weight upon the back of his neck, to which if he yielded in the least, by shrinking downwards, a sharp spike would infallibly run into his chin, which was kept bare for that very purpose.

Barrisdale seems to have struck a commanding figure. He certainly had a good deal of influence amongst his contemporaries but this, as Murray of Broughton pointed out, proceeded 'much more from fear than love'. After the victory at Prestonpans he was dispatched to persuade Lovat to come off the fence:

for such a task, no person was more proper in the whole Rebel army; for tho' he was a blunt man, and of a forbidding utterance, yet he scrupled at saying nothing that might raise the honour of the Highlanders ... Sheridan judged that his bluntness would appear the natural effect of truth without disguise, and add credit to his narration; his devouring looks, his bulky strides, his awful voice, long and tremendous sword, which he generally wore in his hand, with a target and bonnet, edged broad upon the forehead, imparted an awe to the coward and unthinking; while it imprinted a confidence that victory would side with those whom Barisdale should join.

The author of the *Life of Barisdale* also makes it clear just how unpleasant a civil war really was. He implicates both Barrisdales in burning granaries on the north-east coast:

But while Barisdale, the father, destroyed the chief granary in the western corner of the country, Barisdale the son, went with five companies, and set fire to the earl of Sutherland's granaries in the eastern parts, with design to starve the people into an obedience; [Moreover] … the consuming of a granary of meal and barley, was equal to the murdering many poor people, whose lives almost depended upon these.

The same author also claims that Prince Charles was only saved from Barrisdale's treachery by Sheridan's caution and suspicion. Certainly, defeat at Culloden tested the loyalty of the Highland chiefs. With the Prince impotent they were reduced to saving themselves, their estates and their people any way they could. There was much distrust amongst the Jacobites, and both of the Barrisdales as well as Alastair Ruadh of Glengarry were suspected of treachery. Their defeat now allowed the Whig clans to settle old scores:

the militia … was particularly active, and now had it in their power to revenge some family quarrels, and clannish animosities.

A party of the Ross-shire militia, came to Barisdale's house, where they were presented with a sight of the stocks that lay upon a green, opposite to the door, and these they kindled first, then set fire to the house, which was beautifully covered with blue slate, and contained eighteen fire-rooms, besides as many without any chimneys; the flames burnt with great violence, and in a few hours the building was reduced to ashes. A poor revenge to those who had suffered so much in their property by his means, even before the rebellion, and who, during its continuance, had been so much abused by him and his gang.

Both Barrisdales, father and son, were now so much distrusted by the other Jacobites that they were imprisoned in France. After two years in gaol, Coll eventually returned to Knoydart:

but here the face of affairs were changed, for the houses were not only burnt by the militia, but the cattle were driven off.

Coll was arrested again in 1749 and died a prisoner in Edinburgh Castle in 1750. His father died at Barrisdale in 1752.

Despite the ambiguity of some of the evidence, it is clear that Coll's house was at Inverie, probably somewhere near or under the site of the present house. In autumn 1747 David Bruce surveyed the Barrisdale estate and he says that Archibald Macdonell the Elder had his house at Barrisdale, whereas to get to Coll's he had to go through Knoydart. Spanish John confirms this in one of his own footnotes:

> Coll Borisdale's fine stone house of two stories high at Traigh in Knoidart was burnt by ... Captain Ferguson. At Borisdale, old Borisdales's place, the houses were all burnt, the cattle and other effects of the people taken away by the soldiers.

Contemporaries thought Coll's house remarkable because it had two storeys. This made it unique in Knoydart. It was obviously a fine mansion, albeit built with the proceeds of his blackmail.

We also have Captain John Ferguson's own account of the destruction. It comes from a letter written on 12 May 1746 describing the activities of his ship, the *Furnace*, over the previous week.

> ... having gott Information that there was a great many Arms, and Money in McDonalds of Barrasdales house, in Loch Navis, I stood in for it under Spannish Colours, and came to an Anchor within Gun Shott of it; I Landed 120 Men with Orders to burn and destroy the House (which was one of the best in this Country) But before my boats gott on Shore I saw a great Number of Men assembling Armed from all Quarters, that made me wish I had my Men on board again, for they began to fire on the Boats very Briskly. I soon gott a Spring on my Cable, and began firing amongst the Middle of them, which made them retreat with great hast up to the Mountains, but they still Lurked about among Rocks, and fired on my people, but they soon Destroy'd the House, and two or three Villages about it, and not one of them received the Least hurt, altho there were above 300 Armed Men against them; they found in the House 150 Stand of Arms, 130 Cutlasses, 30 Anchors of Brandy, and some small

plunder. But I had the Misfortune to Loose Six of my Men No Body could give me an Account what was become of them; My Lieut is a very Carefull Diligent Officer and Endeavoured all in his power to keep the Men together, But how soon they gott at the Brandy, a great many of them fell to Drinking, which makes me beleive that they either deserted (being all of them Highlanders or Irish Men) or gott Drunk and Stragled from the rest in quest of Plunder.

Curiously, brandy receives no mention in his official log which is more laconic:

of [off] the Laird of Barassdals house at 6 PM firid 48 Guns to beat the House down and Sett the Town on fire and Took 137 Stand of Small Arms.

The *Furnace*, along with other government ships, was cruising off the west coast and bringing the war home to the Jacobites in a manner that had not previously happened.

Macdonald of Scottos

In contrast, we have a very flattering portrait of Donald Macdonald of Scottos, cousin of Coll of Barrisdale. This was penned by the Chevalier de Johnstone, a young gentleman from Edinburgh, who was employed by Lord George Murray and Prince Charles as an aide-de-camp. He formed a close friendship with Macdonald of Scottos during the campaign and later wrote eulogistically of his companion in his *Memoirs*. In March 1746 he describes Scottos's agony on being sent to fight against his son, an officer with the Hanoverian Lord Loudon.

He was a man of about forty years of age, endowed with a fine figure and a prepossessing address, joined to that of an agreeable exterior. He had all the qualities of soul which ordinarily distinguish the honourable and gallant man - brave, polite, obliging, of fine spirit and sound judgement. Although I had not known him but since the commencement of the expedition of the Prince, I soon came to distinguish his merit and the sweetness of his society. I formed with him the closest friendship, notwithstanding the disparity of our ages. He paid back my affection with all the tenderness of a parent. As he was naturally of a gay disposition, I perceived his melancholy on his entering my dwelling. On asking him the cause, this worthy man looked at me, his eyes bathed in tears – 'Ah, my friend, you do not know what it is to be a father. I am of this detachment which must depart this evening to attack Lord Loudon. You do not know that a son whom I adore is with him an officer in his regiment. I believed myself fortunate in obtaining that rank for this dear boy, not being able to foresee the descent of Prince Charles Edward into Scotland. Perhaps tomorrow I shall have the grief to kill my son with my own hand, and that the same ball that I shall fire off in my defence may occasion from myself a death the most cruel! In going with the detachment I may be able to save his life; if I do not march, some other may kill him.' The recital of poor Scothouse rent my heart. I could not refrain from mingling my tears with his, although I had never seen this young man, the subject of the sharp pangs of a tender father. I retained him the whole day at my house, endeavouring to dissipate his fears as much as I possibly could, and making him promise on parting to come straight to my house on leaving the boat. The next day, at evening, I heard a great knock at my door. I ran thither, and perceived the good father holding a young man by the hand, of a jolly figure, who cried to me, his eyes sparkling with joy. 'Behold, my friend, the one who yesterday caused all my alarms. I have taken him prisoner myself; and when I had hold of him he embraced me fervently, not regarding the others who were present.' I then saw him shed tears of joy, very different from those of the night before. We supped all three together at my chamber, and I never had my mind more penetrated with satisfaction than at this supper, by the mutual scene of tenderness between the father and the son ...

Possibly not many of Scottos's own words have survived the conversion to literature, but the portrait is vivid enough. The Chevalier also gives us an idea of the rigours of a campaign in the Scottish Highlands at the end of winter.

> For some time provisions had become very scarce at Inverness; our army suffered severely, and it was badly nourished ... The Prince caused our army leave Inverness on the 13th of April, in order to occupy a position which he had chosen for a field of battle, at a distance of half a league from that city; and we remained there night and day, lying on the ground under the clear sky, without tents or shelter against the inclemency of the weather; the Highlanders having nothing for food but some biscuits and cold water. I kept myself with my friend Scothouse, who parted with me the little victuals which he could get hold of, and giving me equally during the nights, which were very cold, the half of his bed-coverings, and a share of the straw which he had made the Highlanders of his regiment collect.

Eventually, of course, there was a reckoning at Culloden.

> By the unevenness of the marshy ground, our right and the centre were the first to come in contact with the enemy; ... and the left, where I was with Scothouse, was not more than twenty paces from the enemy, who let fly their discharge at the moment when the right began to be on the retreat, and which communicated itself from the right to the left of our army with the quickness of a flash of lightning. ... My unfortunate friend, Scothouse, was killed by my side, without my being so sensibly affected at the moment that I saw him fall, as I have always been since.

He describes the scene again in the second volume of his memoirs.

> My friendship for the unfortunate Macdonald of Scothouse, who was killed at my side at the battle of Culloden, had engaged me to accompany him to the

charge with his regiment. We were on the left of our army, and at the distance of about twenty paces from the enemy, when the rout commenced to become general, before even we had made our charge on the left. Almost at the same instant that I saw poor Scot fall, (the most worthy man that I had ever known, and with whom I had been allied in friendship the most pure from the commencement of the expedition,) to the increase of my horror, I beheld the Highlanders around me turning their backs to fly.

From the Chevalier's account it appears that the left wing had not closed with the enemy before it became apparent that the battle was lost. Those who, like Scottos, were killed must have been cut down by bullets or during the pursuit.

In John Macdonell's autobiography, *Spanish John*, there are a number of footnotes which appeared in its first publication in the *Canadian Magazine* in 1825. John died in 1810 and he certainly wrote some of these notes himself. In one of them he gives a version of the death of Scottos which, whilst not contradicting that of the Chevalier de Johnstone, has a different flavour. Since John was a nephew of Scottos he might have heard the account directly from the two Knoydart men involved. Even allowing for some elaboration it may be broadly true, especially since the same men had been charged with returning some of Scottos's possessions to his wife.

Donald M'Donell, younger of Scottos, was a handsome and well-bred man, romantically brave and highly esteemed by Prince Charles Edward. Many anecdotes are related of his intrepidity and humanity. The morning of the battle of Culloden, a French officer, after viewing the position of both armies, remarked to Scottos that, from the bad position of Charles's army and fewness of their numbers, they must inevitably be defeated, to which Scottos replied that they had only to act as they were ordered. He was of that part of the Highlanders that charged the English line, and when Charles's forces gave way he was led off the field wounded by two of his men. Finding the pursuit coming too close, he desired the men to leave him, as his wound was mortal, and save themselves by flight. Gave them his watch, dirk, purse, etc., to bring home to his wife, and desired them to turn his face to the enemy, that they might not think he was running away. After getting away some distance the men looked behind them and saw the dragoons despatch him.

Even political opponents knew Donald of Scottos by reputation, and accorded him a grudging respect, which was not always furnished to ardent Jacobites. Bruce, describing Scottos in 1750, wrote:

> Here lives also McDonald of Scotas, a near Relation …
> to the present Glengarry. His eldest son who Carried 50
> Men to the Battle of Culloden and was Reckoned the
> most Valiant man of all the McDonalds, together with
> his Lieutenant, Ensign, a Serjeant and Corporal and 18
> Private men were all Killed upon the Spot. I could not
> find that this man or his Father … were in the Least
> Concerned in Thieving.

Similarly, Andrew Fletcher, the Lord Justice-Clerk, wrote in August 1746:

> old Scothouse and his Sons are reckoned the most
> harmless of the theivish Litter of Glengary.

There is a danger of casting the various characters in this drama as heroes or villains. Both Barrisdales appear repulsive. Scottos has been sanctified by martyrdom. The truth is always more complex, particularly in a situation of civil conflict where betrayal was morally relative. Young Archibald Barrisdale had the misfortune to be twice arrested by Ensign Small, an officer in Lord Loudon's regiment who was then stationed at Bernera. It was no mean achievement for a Highlander to be surprised by a Hanoverian, especially twice. It is certainly a great tribute to Small's intelligence and begs the question of how and where he got his information.

Young Ranald Macdonald of Scottos, whose father was killed at Culloden, was also an officer in Lord Loudon's regiment. In later life he had to return to military duties for reasons of finance. In a memorial dated 1796 he refers to a Colonel Small, recently died, who otherwise would have spoken for him. We shall never know the truth behind the many stories of betrayal that so racked the Jacobites in defeat. But we should remind ourselves that as morals are local so they are relative, especially in a civil war. We have the luxury of making judgements from a period of remarkable political consensus. When applied to Jacobite history in the eighteenth century they are of little relevance and less value.

Spanish John

Spanish John is the name given to John Macdonell of Crowlin. He earned it by service with the Spanish army in Italy in 1744–5. In later life he emigrated to America where his children persuaded him to write down his memoirs of his early exploits. He had been sent abroad at the age of twelve to get an education in Rome. His account makes clear how mature and adult the young men of the Highlands were expected to be. He describes his experiences with candour and wry humour, as for instance this scene at a breakfast party:

> Our Hibernian at breakfast got hold of the teapot to help us to some tea, and at the very first motion spilt a tea cupful of that liquor on the calf of the leg of a Mr Ramsay, one of the two gentlemen travellers who had invited us, upon which he started up and took a pretty good dance through the room without any music.

Like all young travellers he met some who would take advantage of him. Here is his report of an encounter with an Irishman called Creach:

> Mr Creach asked me if I would lend him some money. I answered that I was quite a stranger in the country, had no friends, and was afraid I should run short before coming to the end of my journey, and of course could spare none. 'You little puppy,' says Creach, 'I will have it whether you will or not,' at the same time he seized me by the collar; I, as quick as lightning, closed with him, and we had a smart struggle. I was afraid that the fellow would overpower me, but in the nick of time my comrade coming up stairs and seeing my danger, seized Creach by one leg – I was instantly on the top of him, laid both my knees

upon his arms, sat upon his breast, and drew my big French couteau [knife] to cut his throat.

Creach was eventually released unharmed but no doubt shaken. It is unlikely he had met any twelve-year-olds with the spirit of this one from Knoydart. Spanish John then prepared for the next leg of his travels.

O'Rourk told me that he understood by the natives that a wood which lay in our way was much frequented by Robbers, upon which I thought proper to purchase a pair of pistols; and after loading them, gave one to my comrade, M'Donald, telling him that we must fight for our lives if we were attacked, to which he cheerfully assented. We were, however, quite without fear.

Highlanders were brought up to be self-reliant from an early age. The Chevalier de Johnstone has a story about a young boy at the Battle of Prestonpans.

I saw a young Highlander about fourteen years of age, and who was not yet formed, whom some one presented to the Prince as a prodigy for having slain fourteen English soldiers. The Prince asked him if that was true. The young man replied 'that he did not know that he had killed them, but he had knocked down fourteen soldiers with a stroke of his sword'.

School, however briefly attended, always seems to leave an indelible impression on the young mind. Spanish John was no different and he recalled one particular incident well.

Unfortunately for me there was a Maronite, [a Lebanese Christian] … very swarthy, who sat near me upon the uppermost Bench, and while school was in, either through weakness or some other cause, wetted the bench quite close to where I sat; and whispered to one near him that I had done it. Being forbid to speak in the school I waited patiently till the bell rang to dismiss the school for the time; upon the first toll of which I made for the school room door, stood by the side post to wait the coming out of the Maronite who had so grossly belied and affronted

me. Upon his approach I gave him a blow as hard as I
could strike about his upper lip and nose, which produced
a copious discharge of blood ...

The laws of the Roman College punished such offences
with a very rigorous penalty; which was, that the person
... guilty of raising his hand to strike another ... was to
be put into the stocks, hand and feet, and to receive as
many lashes with a cat o'-nine tails upon the back and
shoulders, as should be thought proper ... This
punishment was called a Mule. Next to this for crimes
less atrocious was a Horse. The operation of which was
to stand upon a bucket stool, and to be flogged with a cat
o'-nine tails on the small of the legs

Without hesitation I avowed my guilt, and I was then
told by the Superior that I must undergo the punishment
due to my crime. This I refused to comply with, and said
that such punishments were unworthy of freeborn people.

And in the end he got off scot-free!

Spanish John set off for Scotland at the news of Bonnie
Prince Charlie's adventure, but arrived too late to take part in
the campaign. Some adventures from his colourful early life
feature in his autobiography, which was written many years later
in Canada.

Raonull Mor A' Chrolen

Big Ranald of Crowlin was an illegitimate son of Archibald,
first of Barrisdale. Notices of him appear in both Reverend
Charles Macdonald's *Moidart* and also Fraser-Mackintosh's
Antiquarian Notes. He was evidently something of a character.
Depending on whether you prefer the Fraser Mackintosh or
Macdonald version, Ranald was banished to India for taking
part in the 1745 rising, or Barbados for a brutal murder. During
one or other passage he helped defend the British ship on which
he was travelling from a French attack – an action which
subsequently stood him well with the authorities. On his return
to Scotland he lived at Crowlin which he and his son James
leased along with Scamadale.

Ranald exercised what he probably viewed as his ancestral rights and responsibilities in the heroic manner. According to Charles Macdonald, the parish priest of Moidart:

> It is said that during a certain period of his life Ranald's morals were very weak; and there is a story going that the priest being very indignant at several cases of illegitimacy which, one after the other, were brought before him, and without exception referred to Ranald, went straight to the supposed delinquent and implored him, sarcastically, to make a diligent search through the country, and if he found any more of his offspring to bring them all together, so that they might be baptized with the least possible trouble.

Ranald's energies do not seem to have diminished with time because, at the age of about ninety, he married a Miss Macdonell of Slaney. 'No doubt', says Fraser-Mackintosh charitably, 'to enable the lady to enjoy his pension'.

In politics, Ranald was an lifelong Jacobite.

> When George III expressed, on a certain occasion, a strong desire to see some of the surviving Highlanders who had been out in the '45, a certain number were brought forward, and among them a grim old warrior from Knoydart named Raonull Mor a' Chrolen. After putting some questions to the latter, the king remarked that no doubt he must have long since regretted having taken any part in that **Rebellion**. The answer was prompt and decisive. 'Sire, I regret nothing of the kind.' His Majesty, for an instant, was taken aback at such a bold answer, but was completely softened by the old man adding, 'What I did then for the Prince, I would have done as heartily for your Majesty if you had been in the Prince's place.'

He also possessed a violent temper, which must have made him an intimidating adversary at the time of the Rising.

> During his visits to Rhu [Arisaig], Ranald could scarcely talk of anything except of the Prince, his adventures, and of the great regret which all right-minded persons ought to feel at the failure of the Stuarts to regain their throne.

These topics pre-occupied his mind, even when far advanced in years, viz., when he was over eighty. In his enthusiasm he used to raise his trembling arms, and, in a weak quavering voice, call all to witness that he was still ready to draw the sword and fight for the right cause. On such occasions his sister, losing all patience, used to retort that an army of such warlike veterans as himself would no doubt perform prodigies of valour, but that any general, Whig or Jacobite, would give thanks to heaven that he was not called upon to win victories with them. Nothing brought the old boy's fury to a quicker climax than a remark like this. The veins in his forehead would swell, his lips would tremble, and his features would assume such a ferocious vindictive look, that the late Miss Joanna Macdonald, who in her youth was a frequent witness of such scenes, used to fly from his presence in sheer terror. In his prime Big Ranald was a tall powerfully built man, but his countenance had at all times a harsh and sinister cast about it.

After Culloden

The old order had been defeated on the battlefield, but it was not immediately reconciled to the new. For several years after Culloden, armed bands of Highlanders remained defiant in areas such as Knoydart. The government moved slowly but deliberately, letting time, military pressure and economic circumstances work for them. There were reprisal expeditions by army personnel and Highland militia working for the government. These were often recruited from rival clans, dressed up in uniform and happy to settle old scores. Substantial numbers of cattle were driven away, some Highlanders executed, some transported. Laws were passed; weapons, bagpipes, tartans proscribed. Garrisons were maintained at Fort William and Bernera in Glenelg. The navy reached into every fastness and gradually the diehards were reduced.

Nevertheless, for the government's civilian agents these were uncertain times. As David Bruce said in 1747, they were 'not certain when we lay down but our throatts might be cutt before morning'. Coll Barrisdale had been captured in 1749 and died in Edinburgh Castle in 1750. However, young Archibald Barrisdale, who had also returned to Scotland, remained defiant. Mungo Campbell writes in 1753 that the Knoydart tenants

> have had the Insolence ever since the year 1746 to pay their Rents regularly to the Attainted Barrisdale who since that time absolutely rules them and ranges up and down that Country with a Band of Armed men, dressed as well as himself in the Highland Habite.

'Barrisdale's guard', as it was called, was the last remnant of resistance and it was clear that the government had to reduce it. Archibald was captured soon after Campbell's letter and taken to Edinburgh where he languished in prison under sentence of death. Opposition dwindled away and after 1755 the Commissioners for the Forfeited Estates assumed control. Archibald was not in fact executed but by the time he returned to Knoydart in 1764 he was reconciled to the new order and became a model tenant.

Of all the above characters, so well-known in their day, it is ironic that the one most likely to be remembered is Spanish John, a wanderer who spent much of his life abroad, but whose name lives on, attached to the Knoydart boat.

Chapter 7

A FORFEITED ESTATE

What was life like for the ordinary people of Knoydart in the eighteenth century? We have seen how their owners and landlords fared. But Coll of Barrisdale and Macdonell of Scottos never had to go hungry. They were the select few, just a tiny proportion of the total population; those who controlled the land and dispensed the leases; who owned the cattle, the boats and the principal houses; whose sons and brothers were the priests; who employed the labourers, the craftsmen and the bards. These few families, closely connected by blood to Glengarry, controlled the levers of economic, political, religious and intellectual power. What about the rest of the people?

In 1755 the estate of Barrisdale was forfeited and, until 1784, it was run by the Commissioners for the Forfeited Estates. Their papers provide the single most important body of evidence for the history of Knoydart. For all that forfeiture was a punitive measure it is ironic that these estates were better administered by their conscientious and often progressive government factors than they were before or after. Their administrators were honest by contemporary standards in that they were not out to line their own pockets, perhaps partly because they were subject to scrutiny. The surviving papers include farm surveys, economic reports, estimates, invoices, receipts, lists of tenants, and letters from and by a number of observers over a period of thirty years.

The documents give hard economic evidence for conditions in Knoydart. We learn how they farmed, what they grew, where and how they lived. It is our first such evidence. Using it we can project back to the probable conditions of Knoydart's previous history. It is unlikely that the district's economic base changed greatly since people began to farm here in prehistoric times. We are lucky to glimpse this agricultural society on the eve of its disintegration. By the end of the eighteenth century, sheep runs had become well established in Knoydart and a fragile economic system that had lasted for perhaps 3000 years began to fall apart.

Seen retrospectively, the improvers of the Forfeited Estates were engaged in an uphill struggle. Even after improvement, Knoydart could never sustain itself in competition with other areas which had greater natural advantages. However, using their evidence we can paint a picture of the social economy they found, analyse the changes they made, and assess their net effect. We must also judge their improvements against the harsh fact that within two centuries the indigenous population of Knoydart entirely disappeared. Does this represent failure? These early attempts at improvement also provide a useful benchmark against which to gauge the likely success of similar efforts today.

Why are the Forfeited Estates Papers so important? Because they give us the hard facts and figures of economic life. Not the sunny views of distant literati, not the selfish interests of the owners, but practical, everyday agricultural and human facts about who farmed and where, how and what with. They are also important because without them we might be tempted to view the area very differently. We have two eighteenth-century visions of Knoydart which project it as a land of milk and honey. In one of Mrs Grant of Laggan's *Letters from the Mountains* we find this description dating from 1773. At this stage Mrs Grant was still only eighteen-year-old Anne Macvicar, and her prose was alight with youthful idealism. She knew of

a wondrous region, called Knoidart, where there are no first floors at all, but all is garret, or cellar; inaccessible precipices, overhanging mountains, and glens narrow, abrupt, and cut through with deep ravines, combining with rapid streams, dark pools, and woods so intricate, that the deer can scarce find their way through them. Yet the natives are looked upon as happier than others. Redundant grass and luxuriant

heath afford abundance to their cattle, who are never housed
in winter. Deer, wild fowl, and fish, are in great plenty;
salmon, in particular, crowd their rivers, and shell-fish of all
kinds abound on their rugged coasts. All this they enjoy
without a rival or competitor, for who could go for it, or
carry it away? Bread indeed is a foreign luxury with them,
they raising little or no corn; a ship however comes once or
twice a year, and brings them a supply of meal in exchange
for butter and cheese.

The young authoress thought of Knoydart in terms of a bucolic
idyll. Perhaps if she had visited the district and seen the poverty of
the inhabitants and the squalor of their creel huts, she might have
changed her mind. Alasdair Macdonald, the famous eighteenth-
century Gaelic poet, was also extravagant in his praise of Knoydart:

I went to live at Inverey
A perfect homestead, sappy, dear;
'Tis well-provided, fertile, rich,
Grassy, generous, full of cheer.
Daisies are bursting through its plains,
All crammed with fruit both rich and rare;
No bitter plant yields that dear land,
Crops, honey, milk, and primrose everywhere.
                    (Macdonald, A. and Macdonald, A. *The Poems of
                              Alexander Macdonald*, 1924)

Attractive though these perspectives are, the historian must put
them to one side. They represent a sort of literary mist; idealised,
idyllic and hopelessly unrealistic. They bear no relationship to the
poverty and squalor in which the people of Knoydart actually lived.
Mrs Grant was self-consciously romantic. Alasdair Macdonald is
guilty of the same offence, only slightly mitigated by the fact that
his is in verse. His unqualified praise was partly due to a desire to
discredit his previous home in Eigneig, Moidart, which he had left
under something of a cloud.

We have a different type of account emerging at the very
beginning of the nineteenth century. The following extract is
from a letter written from Fort William in August 1800. The
author is John Leyden whose *Journal of a Tour in the Highlands and*

Western Islands of Scotland was eventually published in 1903.

The shore of Knoydart, along which we sailed, is wild and barren in an eminent degree ... As we entered Loch Nevis the scene was extremely rude and picturesque: projecting rocks and craggy isles threatened to shut up the entrance. As we advanced, the irregular rocks on each side, skirted with heath and covered with gray moss, began to tower in horrid magnificence, till we entered a capacious bason where the estuary through which we had passed expands into a grand extensive lake, on the side of which, lightly shaded with trees, we discovered Scothouse. Here we were hospitably entertained by Mr Gillespie, and took advantage of the presence of Mr MacDonell of Scothouse to enquire concerning the appearance of the country in the first half of the century. Instead of the savage naked appearance which it now presented, Knoydart was formerly clothed with extensive forests, and contained trees of very great magnitude. We learned that the ancient wicker houses of the Highlanders promoted in no inconsiderable degree the destruction of these forests ... At Scothouse Loch Nevis expands into a ample bason, which seems to be entirely encompassed by the bleak circular range of hills in Knoydart and Morar, save at the entrance, where it likewise appears to be shut up by the wild and picturesque hills of Rum and Slate. The view of the lake here is exceedingly wild and romantic. The hills by which it is confined consist entirely of gray rocks and heath, skirted here and there with strips of thin wood where formerly flourished extensive and almost impenetrable forests. ... From Scothouse we sailed up the romantic Loch Nevis ... till our progress was arrested by the tremendous ridge of Mainclach-aird ... We ascended by a winding irregular path into a mountainous pass ... and afterwards began to descend into a small dark vale of black heath, which is certainly as desolate a spot as can be conceived, and where the horrid solitude could only be increased by converting it into a valley of dry bones. The two passes into this horrid vale are blocked up by enormous precipices dreadfully rugged and gray, on the one side irregular and jagged, on the other one vast sheet of shelving rock, from top to bottom patched at intervals with black heath.

Leyden's letter gives us a novel perspective. He is one of the first of a long list of writers and travellers whose journals enticed visitors from their comfortable salons in faraway cities, or sent a frisson down the spines of those not daring to venture among the wild Highlanders. His prose is rather Gothic for modern tastes but reveals the tourist spirit of the day. The area is rugged, there is no doubt about it, and the absence of roads or proper ferries must have made travelling a major ordeal. However, what is not a frightful precipice is still a dreadful declivity and there is more than a little literary pretension in these early accounts. It is ironic that the solitude Leyden found horrid is now protected by all those city-dwellers who fight so ferociously against any new road-development in the Highlands.

These differing views of Knoydart reflect their authors' perspectives. Alasdair Macdonald was a local, fiercely partisan and polemical. Mrs Grant was of Highland descent, sympathetic, enthusiastic and young. Leyden was a visitor, a friend of Walter Scott, with a purpose to his Highland trip. He, along with many early travel writers, adopts a rather self-conscious literary style. As shall become evident from the Forfeited Estates Papers, these projections, although fit to conjure with on a beautiful day in June, would not be a fair summary. They tell us nothing of poverty and degradation, nothing of disease and infant mortality, nothing of toil and travail. If they were true then why did anyone ever leave Knoydart for the New World? Why were farms converted to sheep walks even before the end of the eighteenth century? Unhappily, the gap between a romantic view of the Highland situation and cold reality has persisted to the present day. Literary, cultural and historical projections still serve to obscure a clear view of Highland issues.

A more realistic perspective is provided by David Bruce, who made a general survey of the area in 1750.

All these Countries viz. Knoydart, the Two Morrirs, Moydart, and Arisag, are the most Rough Mountainous and impassable parts in all the Highlands of Scotland, and are commonly called by the Inhabitants of the Neighbouring Countries the Highlands of the Highlands. The People here have very little Corn Land and what they have by Reason of its steepness and Cragginess they are obliged to Dig with the Spade; but the People in these Countries breed prodigious Numbers of Cattle of all kind especially a Sort of Wild Horses which sell very well at the Markets in the Low Country.

William Morison

Some of the most revealing documents in the Forfeited Estates Papers were the farm plans drawn up by William Morison, surveyor. Morison's reports took a common format. He produced a plan drawing, along with a short written summary which included details of the main features of the farm, crops grown and their yield, woodland, names of tenants and level of rent. From the plan itself we can glean invaluable detail such as where the buildings were situated and what dykes were in existence. His sketches also establish farm boundaries and where these were disputed (*See* Plate 7).

Morison commented on the quality of the grazing and gave figures for the quantities of arable land, grassland, rough grazing and woodland. Modern surveying techniques might come up with more exact measurements but there is no doubt from the nature of his report and his careful sketches that he made an honest attempt to survey as accurately as possible. What is striking is the tiny quantity of arable land available in 1771, at a time when the population of Knoydart had probably already reached its peak, and just before large-scale emigration began to take place. What Morison marked as arable ground probably represents virtually the maximum extent of what was ever tilled in Knoydart. His figures give the proportion of arable ground as only *1 acre in every 200* on the Barrisdale estate. Even allowing for the fact that Glengarry's property in Knoydart was reckoned to be of better quality it is unlikely that the total proportion of arable land in Knoydart ever approached one per cent. This single fact explains much of Knoydart's economic history. By contrast, in about 1750, David Bruce wrote of three neighbouring parishes in Easter

Ross that they 'look like one Continued Field of Corn'.

The following extracts from the Forfeited Estates Papers are chosen to illustrate particular themes. In some instances I have supplemented these with material from elsewhere in order to paint a more complete picture. These contemporary reports speak for themselves but I refer readers to the Reading List for information on where to find further analyses.

Farming

This estate ... being very mountaineous and rocky ... is only fit for pasture and the rearing of black cattle, and there being very little or no arable ground, the inhabitants live chiefly upon the product of their cattle. They, however, sow a little grey oats and barley and the raising of potatoes is much attended to by the whole inhabitants.

As the estate is in the neighbourhood of Lochurn, where herring and other fish always abound, and that each boll of oats or barley sown yields about double the quantity of increase that is generally reapt in other parts of the Highlands, it yielding about six bolls for every boll sown, the inhabitants have bread all winter and spring in small quantities, being in these seasons supplied with fish, potatoes and a little beef, butter and cheese ... Their black cattle and sheep feed in the hills all the seasons in the year and are never put within a house ... The manure chiefly made use of are sea weeds and ferns ... There is no grass seed sown upon this estate nor any hay made upon it, nor are there any inclosures or march dykes upon it, the boundaries of the farms being only known by custom and tradition.

The people, for the most part of the summer and harvest seasons, repair from the lower parts, or those next to the sea, of their farms to the tops of the hills, which are in winter inaccessible, and in these seasons they convert what of their cattle milk is not consumed for their present support into butter and cheese, part of which they then dispose off and export to Slate ... and import in place of it oat meal for their present support, but they sell no other butter and cheese than for this purpose, but

sell as much of their black cattle to drovers from the south
countrys as generally pays their rent.

(Mungo Campbell, 1755–6)

All the Cornland on Barrisdale is taken in from the hill – of
a gravelly soil, delved with the Spade, manured with Sea-
wreck or Ferns, and cropp'd with black Oats. They have no
Ploughs, Limestone or Marle on the estate and grind their
corn on the Quern.

(William Morison, 1771)

One problem associated with Knoydart's relatively primitive
agricultural practice was that ground had to be left fallow to recover
from tillage. In Skiary the cornland was 'cropp'd two years with Oats,
then allowed to rest for four Years'. In Muinal also two years of oats
were followed by grass. Of the latter farm Morison adds

There is plenty of Potatoe plots in the most convenient
places, raised in the lazy bed way which are sown the year
following with Oats.

The same seems to have happened at Riguel.

The Barrisdale estate was generally regarded as less profitable
than other parts of Knoydart:

The tenants of Glengary raise as much grain, as is sufficient
to maintain their families, whereas every tenant on
Barrisdale, excepting the farm of Torcruin, is obliged to buy
meal for their support.

(William Morison)

In this context it is perhaps significant that Torcruin only had one
tenant.

In Knowdort the inhabitants dwell in villages bordering on
the sea, along the sides of Lochurn and Lochneavis; here the
soil is in general light, yielding crops of barley, oats, and potatoes.
The hills, though high, are mostly green to the top, and afford
excellent pasture for all kinds of cattle.

The oats are commonly sown in the latter end of March
and beginning of April; immediately thereafter the potatoes
are planted, and then the barley. … but owing to the deluges

of rain that too often fall about this season of the year, the hay as well as other crops are often not secured till November. Grazing seems to be the only kind of farming for which this country is adapted; from necessity, and not choice, agriculture is carried on; the frequent rains, together with the inundations of the rivers, prove so destructive as to render the crops sometimes insipid and useless; but the price of meal ... will still urge them to continue their old method of farming with all its disadvantages, it being impossible to purchase the quantity required at such exorbitant prices. In the most favourable seasons, the crops raised are barely sufficient for the maintenance of their families during three-fourths of the year; ... The cows in this parish are of a good kind, well shaped and piled, and being seldom housed, very hardy.

(OSA – Parish of Glenelg by
Rev Colin Maciver, Minister, 1793)

Cattle-raising

Like other mountain peoples the Highlanders practised transhumance. Essentially this means moving livestock to the hill pastures during the high summer to maximize the grazing potential of the land. It is normally the case that stock would then be wintered on lower ground, but as we shall see this did not always happen in Knoydart. According to Morison the farm of Inverie had the best shieling in Glen Guseran, at Breakachy, where they lived for three months of the year.

They are good managers of cattle, which are esteemed of a quality equal to any of the West Highlands. ... Their grass, where best managed, is divided into summer, harvest, winter and spring grasses, which is laid out in some parts in districts. ... They have the grass for each season divided into as many divisions as it will admit of, as they look upon it [as] of consequence to change their grass often. ... It is remarkable the skill they show in chusing their pasturages for the different seasons. It is not the local situation but the quality of the grasses they study. Every farmer is so far a botanist as to distinguish

the particular season each grass is in perfection. I have
seen some of their wintering ground very high and
exposed and at a very great distance from the sea, when
at the same time they had grasing close by the sea and
where no snow lay in winter. Yet the quality of the grass
as winter grass determined them to chuse the high,
stormy country.

From what I have said above it will appear that the
tenents in that part of the country are very attentive to
the management of their cattle, which is the principal
thing worthy of attention there, as their climate and soil
are against agriculture.

(Archibald Menzies, 1768)

Manual Labour

There is not a plough used on the whole of this estate
except at Inveruie. The inhabitants labour their land by
turning the earth with spades, nor in most of the farms is
it possible, from the ruggedness of the ground, which
abounds with boggs and precipies, to yoke a horse to any
work, whereby the lands must want manure, except what
is carried on men's backs, in which manner they are
likewise in most of the farms oblidged to lead their fireing,
being turff and wood.

(Mungo Campbell)

The farms ... generally ly [by] the sides of the lochs, the
arable parts mostly steep and rocky and delved with the cash
crom, which is a crooked spade well calculated for stony
ground. I am informed some people will delve an acre in
a day with it.

(Archibald Menzies)

Bread-making

There are no milns [mills] in this country, nor do they
ever prepare the little grain they reap in the ordinary
manner, but set fire to the sheaves until the stalk and the
grain are separated and then they gather what of the grain
remains unburnt, which they grind with a hand

instrument made for that purpose called a quearn, which produces a sort of coarse meal, very bad in appearance but which the natives reckon better than any other!

(Mungo Campbell)

They retain the barbarous custom of burning their straw in making graddan meal ... From shearing their corns they will make bread in a few hours. They reckon this meal much better than any other for making their eynirich or broth and water gruel, and suppose it a preservative against the flux, to which they are much subject all alongst this coast.

(Archibald Menzies)

Forestry

The free grazing of cattle, and particularly goats, damaged the young trees. Visiting fishermen also damaged the woodland.

The wood upon this estate is very invalueable [i.e. not valuable] in any other respect than for the conveniency of the natives to support their buildings and supply them with fireing. The whole consists of birch and alderwoods growing in inaccessible parts, except that of the farms of Camusdoun and Skiarree upon the coast of Lochurn, where formerly there was a fir wood but for some time has been wholly destroyed by vessels fishing for herring in Lochurn.

(Mungo Campbell)

There are some woods upon the sides of Loch Urin and Loch Nevish which, if properly cared for, might turn to account. They should be inclosed with sufficient stone dykes, the hazles cut down, the vacancies in the wood filled up with oak etc, no cattle to be allowed to enter them and goats to be banished the barony.

(Archibald Menzies)

Fishing

They are in the center of the herring lochs, being near to the south side of Sky, where the greatest fishing have been for some years past ... Besides, herring of a very good quality and in great quantities are frequently caught in Lochs Urin & Nevish.

The herring caught here are very fine. The course they generally come is reckoned from the westward by Barra and betwixt Canna and Skye. In the inner Loch Nevish they have always herring, but it is so deep that they can only catch them with the couraguan or drift shot. They have plenty of haddocks, whiting etc. and summer cod.

(Archibald Menzies)

The great support the tenants of Barrisdale have, is the herring fishing on the Lochs Urn and Nevis, which begins in the Dog days, and continues to the end of December. The country people seldom have Casks or Salt, therefore they sell them fresh to the Bounty Men, from 8d to 4 shillings the Barrel. They cure as many fish for their families, as will serve them ¾ of the year. The herring are boiled with Potatoes, and their Butter, Cheese & Milk maintain them the remaining part of the year.

(William Morison)

Education

There is neither a parochial school nor charity school ... in all Knoydart ... There is not above four or five persons on the estate of Barrasdale that speak English and but three can read or write.

(Mungo Campbell)

In Knowdort, there is one of the Society schools; the teacher has a salary of £12 Sterling allowed him; and scholars are from 30 to 40 in number.

(OSA)

Houses

The whole houses of the country are made up of twigs manufactured by way of creels called wattling and covered with turff. They are so low in the roof as scarce to admitt of a person standing in them, and when these are made up with pains they endure ten or twelve years. They thatch them [with] rushes.

(Mungo Campbell)

There are Six Creel houses on this farm [Riguel] not-withstanding they have plenty of Stone to build stone houses.

(William Morison)

It is clear from Morison's report that, even in 1771, the settlements on Loch Nevis still clung to their primitive housing. The three farms of Riguel (Reidh a Ghuail), Brunsaig (Braomisaig) and Sallachry (Salach-airigh) had 28 houses between them. Twenty-seven were creel, one was stone.

Whisky

The inhabitants are in winter taken up in looking after their black cattle and preparing their ground for a little grey oats, barley and potatoes, and some of them in fishing for herring, and in summer and harvest they are generally very idle, having nothing to do but to herd their cattle and keeping their hutts in repair. There are neither maltmakers nor stills on the estate, but there are two whisky houses, one at Sorious [Sourlies] and the other at Inveruie, who import whisky from a place in the neighbourhood of Inverness called Ferintosh, from whence also all Lochaber, Moydart, Arisaig, Moror and Glengarry are supplied with whisky, which is drunk in great abundance by the inhabitants, and the multiplicity of whisky houses is one great means of the poverty of the inhabitants.

(Mungo Campbell)

Fuel

The tenants of Inveruie cut their Peats on the West side of this farm [Miolary], it lies disadvantageous on account of the distance and carriage as few of them have horses and their servants are under the necessity of carrying them home on their backs in Creels this piece of Labour consumes much of their time.

> [of Achgline, up the River Carnach] the roots of fir-
> trees, which are dug out of the Moss are burnt as fuel,
> when the Season for casting Peats is rainy.
>
> (William Morison)

The overall context for the work of the Forfeited Estates factors in Knoydart was what historians call the Agricultural Revolution. Improvement was everything, an intellectual obsession as much as a set of practical schemes. Armed with a raft of ideas which had proved successful elsewhere, these enterprising agents from the more advanced areas of Scotland set about bringing the Highlands into their brave new World. The problem was that conditions in the north-west were very different.

The improvers had a long catalogue of ills which they perceived in Highland agricultural practice. These issues recur again and again throughout the documents. If we analyse them one by one we should be able to determine whether improvement was, as they firmly believed, the answer to Highland problems; or whether in fact they were swimming against an economic tide. A tide which, two centuries later, still presses inexorably on what is left of Highland agriculture in favour of more fertile soils in gentler climes with longer growing seasons.

First, the improvers were unhappy at the absence of ploughs and horses. Inverie was the only farm on the whole estate where a plough was used. It was not that other farmers in Knoydart preferred the backbreaking labour associated with their special dog-legged foot spade or *cas-chrom*; it was simply that it was more economic. In very few places on the west coast north of Kintyre is there enough flat arable ground to warrant a wooden plough with horses. The *cas-chrom* is much more efficient for the tiny patches of fertile ground that were scattered between rocks and bogs. John Leyden writes of hillsides near Crinan in Argyll:

> Almost every spot of arable land appeared cultivated, even where no plough could possibly be employed. On enquiry we found that the spade was used in tillage where the country is very rocky and irregular.

The improvers also moaned about the 'barbarous habit' of graddan wheat, which is where the husks were burned off in a fire. No, it was not an ideal method, but it is debatable whether proper mills could ever be an economic proposition in much of the Rough Bounds. Tiny communities of two or three families were scattered in every bay and inlet, separated from each other by rugged coasts and turbulent seas. Taking corn elsewhere to be ground must have seemed a dubious proposition. Life was full of risks without adding unnecessarily to them.

March dykes were an article of faith with the improving factors. Time and again there is reference to disputes between the tenants and the need for proper marches. Indeed, one of the main purposes of Morison's survey was to plan the most sensible course for dykes. We glimpse a previous system in his comment that

> The people of Inveruie say that in the old times there was no fixed march between them and the tenants of Scotus.

The improvers, however, were interested in individual, not communal, solutions. Over the next century these march dykes were built, followed in the last decades of the nineteenth century by wire fences. What good did they do? Yes, they settled disputes, but in the end these miles and miles of dyke, representing thousands and thousands of man-years of labour, are they not just a monument to wasted industry?

If we take the longer view, what really affected Highland agriculture were the commodity prices of corn and kelp, sheep and cattle. These were factors over which neither the Knoydart farmers, nor the improvers, had any control. The droving trade in cattle and sheep had started before the process of improvement, and continued long afterward. Its ups and downs depended not so much on particular events in Knoydart as on large-scale external forces like the economic consequences of war with France.

Some of the improvers' ideas may have had practical benefits. In particular, they were appalled by the housing conditions they met on the Barrisdale Estate. In the Rough Bounds, 'creel huts' were the norm. These consisted of small roundish huts with walls and roof made of wattle and turf. They only lasted a few years and the small-scale version that did for a shieling probably only one summer. They were unhygienic, squalid and offered little more than shelter from the weather. The improvers encouraged the building of proper stone houses and even before 1784 saw some success. Within the following century, stone became the norm.

There is no way to quantify the effect of this improvement on the living standards and therefore the longevity of the occupants. Nevertheless, stone houses probably increased comfort, improved health and reduced infant mortality. Against this we must recognise that creel huts were within the means and ken of the local people. They could build them themselves, with local resources and individual effort. As stone house-building became standard practice so local families found they lacked the capital and skills necessary. Masons had to be employed, roofing timbers had to be bought. Increasingly, this required a capital commitment from the landlord, who, of course, looked for a return from his money.

The Forfeited Estates factors also tried to open up the communications network. Any improvements to the tracks that linked settlements to each other and beyond were welcome. The building of a bridge at Inverie must have greatly benefited the inhabitants. Ironically, the lack of communications with the outside world later became one of Knoydart's principal selling points. When contrasted with the fortunes of Morar, Arisaig and Moidart to the south it appears that this lack of communication was probably one of the reasons for the community's ultimate demise.

It is difficult to make fair judgements at a distance of two centuries, but looking at the West Highlands today perhaps some of the improvement schemes were wasted. The improvers may have judged the previous agricultural practice of the Knoydart people too harshly. What seemed barbarous may in fact have been reasonably efficient in the circumstances, substituting human labour for the capital they lacked and adopting an older community-based pastoral system in contrast to the new individual tenant-farmer paradigm proselytised by the improvers. It is a conflict that has been repeated all round the world ever since.

The 'economic' approach adopted by the improvers was inevitable. But, in an environment as harsh as the Highlands, once you practise farming primarily to pay a money rent to a landlord, as opposed to raising food for your family and a local laird, then you have started down a road that leads to emigration or clearance. The people of Knoydart always retained something of the hunter-gatherer from their prehistoric forebears. Nature did provide some alternatives when the crops failed. The sea could be fished, the shore could be combed for shellfish, deer could be hunted, birds and their eggs eaten. Fuel was free in the form of trees and peat. The raw materials for housing could be provided locally, they did not have to brought in from outside. Their distance from markets and mills made them look for small-scale local solutions to problems, solutions that may not have been inefficient. Certainly, they made excellent use of their cattle-grazing grounds. Their continued occupation of creel huts may have been due to a combination of ignorance, habit and lack of capital.

During the second half of the eighteenth century the people of Knoydart became interdependent with the outside world. They became less of a self-enclosed community, increasingly locked into the great economic web without. In good years this served them well; they benefited from rising prices for cattle and kelp in the Napoleonic wars. But in times of hardship this mighty economic wheel ground them down and broke them. They could not remain immune from such a potent system. People will always be drawn by the prospect of higher living standards, and the critical prices were now set in distant markets. The poor people of a remote and primitive peninsula were powerless once they had been taken up by the great juggernaut of capitalist enterprise that was eighteenth and nineteenth-century Britain. The owners of the land wanted a return on what they now regarded as their capital.

Chapter 8

THE POPULATION PROBLEM AND EMIGRATION

Since the eighteenth century there has been a population problem in Knoydart. The issue came to public attention in the 1770s – and has remained there ever since. Its symptoms have been poverty, clearance and emigration, which to this day are matters of passionate political and economic debate. Before the eighteenth century we have no evidence for local population levels but it may well be that the problem was endemic, only coming to the public eye after 1773.

The Sources
Our earliest population figures for Knoydart come from the mid-eighteenth century. This was the period during which Dr Webster conducted his census of Scotland and there was a growing interest in population statistics. In the past, such figures had been collected for purposes of taxation or military levy; now it was also for their economic, social or religious implications. We have Dr Webster's estimate for 1755, Bishop Hugh Macdonald's for 1764, Reverend J Walker's figure for 1765 and Reverend Colin Maciver's in 1793. For the period 1800–1831 we have the results of four decennial census returns, which give figures for the whole of Glenelg rather than Knoydart specifically. By comparing them with Reverend Maciver's figure for 1793, which also applied to the whole parish, we can make a fairly accurate projection of the figure for Knoydart.

From 1841 to 1891 we have six more detailed census returns which allow us to place people in their actual settlements. Making use of all these figures we can plot the population from 1755 to 1900, the period of demographic crisis (*See* Figure 4). In these years the population of Knoydart reached an historical peak. This, coupled with something of a revolution in Highland agricultural practice, resulted in the trauma of emigration and clearance. After 1853, the local population went into irreversible decline and, instead of being self-sustaining, Knoydart became economically dependent on the outside world. This period, therefore, represents a watershed in the area's history.

General causes

Knoydart did not face this problem alone. In general terms, there was a large rise in Highland population during the latter part of the eighteenth century. Despite clearance and emigration it continued to rise in the early nineteenth century, peaked around the decade 1831–1841 and declined thereafter. Various causes have been offered, such as the ending of clan warfare, the introduction of potatoes, rising kelp and cattle prices during the Napoleonic wars and vaccination against smallpox. Unfortunately, none of these provide a satisfactory explanation of why Knoydart's population was already 1000 in 1764. We must look to the first half of the century for the causes of the increase – or possibly earlier still. The problem became apparent to the outside world after 1773; it may have existed locally a long time before this.

Although most of the Highlands experienced population increase, the responses to its consequent problems varied from district to district. Clearance and emigration were common solutions, but few areas have suffered to quite the extent of Knoydart. In searching for reasons as to why ordinary Highlanders were such *victims* of change, attention has sometimes focused on the political vacuum caused by the government's repressive measures after 1745. Certainly the relationship between chief and clansmen changed irreversibly during this period. However, despite the social, economic and legal consequences of the failure of the Jacobite Risings, they were essentially a political diversion. The population crisis, clearance and emigration would still have occurred either if the 1745 had not happened or if the Stuarts had regained the throne. Fundamental economic dilemmas still had to be resolved and, in the contemporary political climate, it is difficult to see how this could have happened except through painful economic and social dislocation. A political vacuum in the Highlands did not cause the problem – although it may have rendered Highlanders less able to cope with it.

The Highlanders operated, and had done for hundreds, perhaps thousands of years, a primitive pastoral economy. They grew what crops their climate and soils would allow; they exploited the sea – but only so far as their immediate needs dictated – and they kept what cattle their hills would support. There was a natural balance in this. If the equilibrium was upset by bad harvests, disease or scarcity then their numbers reduced or they stole what they needed from elsewhere. They exchanged any surplus products for items they required but could not produce themselves. This system remained relatively unchanged from the time people first began to hunt, gather or farm in the Highlands.

What happened during the period 1750–1850 is that this primitive economic engine began to crash out of gear. Some of the factors were internal, many more were external. Agricultural practice was transformed by the introduction of the potato, probably by about 1740. The land now produced more food and could support more people. At the same time, the failure of Jacobitism involved the Highlands in a period of economic reprisal and political repression. Surplus manpower began to be seen as a liability rather than an asset. In the latter half of the eighteenth century, money rents became increasingly important to landowners. As they applied upward pressure on rents, so sheep began to be preferred to people. Towards the end of the century, inoculation against smallpox dramatically reduced the death rate. Cattle and kelp prices rose and fell dramatically during and after the Napoleonic wars. The Highland economy, instead of being relatively self-contained, became increasingly dependent on external factors such as fluctuating values for kelp, cattle and sheep.

Unfortunately, these broad economic factors worked their social effects in a clumsy and haphazard way. Harvest failure gave no warning of itself, any more than falling prices for cattle and kelp after the battle of Waterloo and the ending of the Napoleonic wars. The herring might appear in armies one year, in companies the next. The structure of the Highland, indeed the Scottish economy, was not such as to allow rapid redeployment of resources to even out the worse effects of recession or natural disaster. It lacked flexibility and resilience. Numerous topographical accounts by eighteenth-century visitors to the Highlands make this vulnerability clear. In bad seasons there was starvation; in good years there was a surfeit that could not be stored. Furthermore, the contemporary moral climate was only beginning to cope with the economic and social changes that were transforming Britain. Christianity had always favoured maintaining the poor, but the Highland economy was uniform, fragile and unresilient. Economic mishaps which affected the whole area made charity irrelevant by the sheer scale of the problem. The contemporary capacity for relief was restricted to maintaining a small proportion of the old, sick or incapable.

There were few towns in the Highlands, few artisans, no merchant or professional classes, no industrial labour force. Society was still cast in a heroic frame. There were landowners, landholders and the landless. There were almost no other social groups apart from the odd specialist craftsman. Whilst couching the problem in these general terms, we should specify that we are dealing with Knoydart as part of the 'Highlands of the Highlands'. Not all areas behaved in exactly the same manner. Local circumstances and conditions modified the particular application of general rules. Kintyre, for instance, progressed differently, saved by its richer agricultural land and the burgh of Campbeltown. In areas such as Bonawe, Furnace and Invergarry, local conditions were affected by the presence of iron smelters. The lead mines in Strontian, the building of the Caledonian Canal, the presence of the garrison town of Fort William, road-building projects; all of these generated local effects. The only exceptional factor in Knoydart was herring. Vast shoals came to Lochs Nevis and Hourn – but erratically. The Highlanders did not have the resources to take advantage of this natural bounty in the same way as fishing boats from other parts of Scotland. There was little or no salt to preserve the fish and most locals fished purely to satisfy their short-term needs. This failure to develop a fishing industry has always been one of the conundrums of Highland history.

It is difficult to assess the maximum population figure that Knoydart could support by its own efforts and the available natural resources. Throughout its early history there must have been some sort of Malthusian relationship between population and resources. When a population outran its food supply it either had to steal or starve. Highland history is littered with examples of both outcomes, although starvation tended to be private and unnoticed whereas predation led the Highlanders into general obloquy. The *creach* was a systematic and perennial response to the problem of food shortage. From the islands they raided Ireland, from the mainland they ravaged the Eastern or Lowland plain. In Knoydart's case, they may have reached both.

Eventually, political changes ended these Highland solutions to the problem of food supply. After the Union of Crowns in 1603 predation in Ireland was no longer an option. From the Civil Wars of the seventeenth century until Culloden in 1746 the Highlanders experienced, or enjoyed, a century of political turmoil. As the dynastic struggle was eventually resolved so predation on the Lowlands – and even other parts of the Highlands – became increasingly restricted. That the good people of Knoydart relied on this expedient to maintain themselves is suggested by two facts. First, by Barrisdale's blackmail operation in the 1730s and 1740s, where he maintained his tenants by offering protection in return for food – in this case 'black meal'. Secondly, by a letter dated 23 March 1745 at Mugstot, Skye, from Sir A Macdonald to Macleod where the writer complains that

> there has been a small invasion from Knoydart; they carried off three cows; as their boat was small, left the guts.

Political and military repression after Culloden ended cattle-theft on the grand scale as practised by Barrisdale. For the rest of Scotland this was a blessing. For the people of Knoydart it was mixed.

Between 1750 and 1850 any previous equilibrium between people and food supply became increasingly disturbed. Population levels rose markedly and people grew dependent on potatoes. The potato is one of the few crops to thrive in Highland conditions and was also valued for its utility in breaking new ground. It was probably introduced to Knoydart about 1740. By 1841 its high yield had made it the staple for huge numbers of poor Highlanders. Yet within a few years the whole crop failed due to blight – causing untold misery and destitution. The potato famine did not bring the mass starvation in Scotland that it wrought in Ireland, but its economic consequences were enormous. It broke the back of many Highland communities and it is no coincidence that the Knoydart Clearance followed in 1853.

Population levels and the economic variables each followed their own cycles. When there was a sharp disjunction between the two then Highland communities faced enormous stresses. Kelp and cattle prices had soared during the Napoleonic wars, allowing Highlanders to sustain higher living standards on the same output. Once the wars had ended, these prices collapsed, with dire effects throughout the region. Opportunities for employment as soldiers fluctuated with the outbreak of war or peace. The proposed mass emigration of the Glengarry Fencibles with Father Alexander Macdonell in 1802 was in direct response to the disbandment of the regiment.

This relationship between population levels and external economic factors was far too volatile. When the fishing was good and kelp and cattle prices high then a population could be supported, children fed and rents paid. But there was no mechanism for absorbing shocks when things went wrong. There was little flexibility in the Highland economic structure, a situation that persists today. If we compound several separate problems we get a disaster, made more acute by a bad, greedy or incompetent landlord. The situation in Knoydart was worsened by the staggering debt of the Glengarry family. The frailties of this anachronistic type of landlordism dragged the people down with it. The old relationships broke down irretrievably, in the economic, if not yet in the cultural sphere. The clan's previous military function was not sustained, although service in the army or fencible regiments brought short-term relief.

The fishing industry also suffered from volatility. In the years of plenty, every family who lived by the shore could put aside some barrels of herring for winter consumption. The biggest problem was usually the supply of salt for their preservation. Unfortunately, the herring could never be depended upon. Some years they visited Lochs Nevis and Hourn in their millions, in other years they were conspicuous by their absence. The fragility of the Highland economy is demonstrated by the wild fluctuations between feast and famine. From the mid-eighteenth century the years of scarcity began to be recorded by visitors when previously they had escaped attention. In 1771–2, and again in 1782–3, there was crop failure followed by severe privation. All agricultural economies face the problem of harvest failure. In the Highlands, agriculture has always been so marginal that the risk factor was higher than elsewhere. In 1836, Reverend Alexander Beith wrote of the parish of Glenelg:

> such quantities of rain fall, and at all seasons, that an agriculturalist might calculate on losing almost every fourth crop.

When crops failed people had to fall back on fishing, but neither could this be relied upon. Reverend Beith added:

> but, of late years, the fishing has failed, as on all the west coast of Scotland, to the impoverishment of a large population who subsisted by it.

Shellfish

It is difficult for us to appreciate just how close the poor in eighteenth-century Scotland were to starvation. During such periods many throughout the north and west were driven to live off shellfish from the beach. The author of the *Life of Barisdale* painted a picture of desperation amongst the poor Highlanders of the north-east:

> for it is well known, that from the month of March, to the middle of August, some poor upon the coast, have

nothing but shell-fish, such as muscles, cockles, and the like, to support them. Poverty reigns so much among the low class, that scarce a smile is to be seen in their faces.

Once the previous year's surplus was consumed they were reduced to scratching for a living along the shore, dependent on shellfish just like their Stone Age ancestors. It was the same, or worse, on the west coast. Pennant paints a similar picture of Skye in 1772:

the poor are left to Providence's care: they prowl like other animals along the shores to pick up limpets and other shell-fish, the casual repasts of hundreds during part of the year in these unhappy islands. Hundreds thus annually drag through the season a wretched life: and numbers, unknown, in all parts of the western highlands ... fall beneath the pressure, some of hunger, more of the putrid fever, the epidemic of the coasts, originating from unwholesome food, the dire effects of necessity.

Near Barrisdale we find the placename Camusnacroggan. The second element may be a corruption of Gaelic *creachag* (cockle) or *creachan* (clam). Doubtless, this beach earned its name from being a natural larder for the poor of Knoydart during the long and bitter winters. If the harvest was meagre, or the herring were scarce, then shellfish were all that lay between them and starvation. In times of dearth the Highlanders had no alternatives to fall back upon. There were no trades that could be turned to, no factories to absorb labour, no mines or craftshops.

In his autobiography, Spanish John writes:

At Borisdale ... the houses were all burnt, the cattle and other effects of the people taken away by the soldiers. An old woman remarked to the plundering party that although they took all moveables, they could not take away the strand which abounded in shell-fish, and upon this the party ploughed up the strand; to such a pitch of inveteracy were things carried on.

The match of style and spellings with the main body of the text argue that this note is by Spanish John himself and records a

Figure 4: Population Statistics: Knoydart (district) and Glenelg (parish)

Knoydart is part of Glenelg parish so figures for the latter include Knoydart and North Morar.

| | Knoydart (district) | | | | | | | | Glenelg (parish) | | | | | | | |
Year	Houses	Families	Ave House	Males	Females	(%)F	Age<20 %	Total	Houses	Families	Ave House	Males	Females	(%)F	Total	Source
1755							(50) a	827 c							1816	Webster
1764								960								Bishop Hugh Macdonald
1765								912								Walker
1783								1042								Bishop Alexander Macdonald
1788								500 + children								Mr Austin Macdonald
1793							(49) b	1000								OSA
1800									528	528	5.4	1358	1476	(52)	2746	Census
1811									501	516	5.2	1216	1395	(53)	2834	Census
1821									471	471	6.0	1374	1433	(51)	2611	Census
1831									508	511	5.7	1367	1507	(52)	2807	Census
1841	155	156	6.0	447	481	(52)		928							2874	Census
1851	165	170	5.5	410	503	(55)	52	913								Census
1861	103	111	5.6	261	313	(55)	43	574								Census
1871	88	91	5.6					491								Census
1881	87	91	5.2	206	206	(50)		456								Census
1891	96	96	4.3					412								Census

a 50% of Barrisdale estate in 1755 were under seventeen.

b 49% of Glenelg district were under the age of twenty in 1793.

c A comparison of Webster's figures for Ardnamurchan and Glenelg with surveys done in 1764 and 1774 suggests that he included North Morar in Ardnamurchan rather than Glenelg. This means that the figure of 827 Papists refers to the population of Knoydart.

Figure 5: Eviction and Emigration from Knoydart

Year	Number	Ship	Location	Source
1773	425	*Pearl*	Including Knoydart	McLean
1786	(540)/604	*Macdonald*	Knoydart	(Fraser-Mackintosh)/Austin Macdonald (priest)
1790	6	*British Queen*	Invernguseran	Bumsted Appendix B List VII
1793	some		Knoydart	McLean
1770-93	800		Knoydart	Old Statistical Account
1801	4	*Dove*	Knoydart	Passenger-list
1801	12	*Sarah*	Knoydart	Passenger-list
1802	1		Knoydart	Somerled Macmillan
1802	600 + 105	*Neptune* +?	Loch Nevis, including Knoydart	Bumsted Appendix A Table 1
1804	11 families (55)		Ridarroch, Doun, Airor, Kyles	Fraser-Mackintosh
1806	1 family (5)		Derryverigyle	Fraser-Mackintosh
1808	10 families (50)		Skiary, Sandaig, Airor, Sourlies	Fraser-Mackintosh
1815	12 families (60)		Knoydart	McLean
1819	1 family (5)		Knoydart	McLean
1811-21	(1389)		Glenelg parish including Knoydart	1821 Census
1822	5		Knoydart	McLean
1831	5		Knoydart	McLean
1821-31	many families	*Tamerlane*	Glenelg parish including Knoydart	1831 Census
1835	1 family (5)		Airor	1894 William Macinnes
1837	7		Knoydart	McLean
1852	7	*Lord Warriston*	Knoydart	R MacIsaac, Australia
1853	332	*Sillery*	Knoydart	1894 Gillies MacIsaac

Average household size in Knoydart between 1841 and 1881 was between five and six, and the ratio of families to houses was almost 1 to 1. For the purpose of estimating numbers of emigrants, I have assumed an average family size of five. This matches well with M McLean's estimate of 4.6 to 5.7.

Given the difficulties of matching the different figures, we can do no more than estimate the number of emigrants from Knoydart in the period 1773–1853 (eighty years) as between 2000 and 2500.

contemporary story. It seems rather partisan, especially since it is difficult to imagine any body of soldiers going to the trouble of doing something as pointless as ploughing up a beach for spite. It is more likely that they too were digging the strand for shellfish, perhaps doing it in a systematic manner by using agricultural implements. To the people of Barrisdale, watching from a safe distance, it was an opportunity for a good story and a little revenge.

By the eighteenth century there was a greater awareness of what was going on in the peripheral areas of Britain. Communications were better, both physical and literary, and Highland economic problems began to register on the public mind. In previous centuries the old, the weak, the young, just quietly, meanly, died. From the eighteenth century their plight began to be recognised, if not always alleviated. Unfortunately, when the Highland economy was in trouble some observers saw it simply in terms of overpopulation, the answer to which was emigration or clearance.

Overpopulation is not a fixed quantity. In today's world it is not regarded as sufficient just to feed people. They must be clothed and housed and offered reasonable living standards. In 1764 all needs beyond food were fairly basic; people could be housed and clothed with locally available raw materials. An acceptable living standard was seen simply in terms of adequate food and shelter. As time passed, so expectations rose. Part of the pressure for emigration was undoubtedly economic betterment. This must have increased as the gap between the lifestyle that could be sustained in the barren Highlands was compared to that which beckoned in the New World. Certainly a good deal of the early emigration from Knoydart was voluntary.

Distribution

Unfortunately, we cannot simply project back from the 1841 census to find the previous settlement pattern because Knoydart's population distribution had already been modified by 'improvement'. As early as 1764, tenants were evicted from Carnoch to make way for Archibald Macdonald of Barrisdale. In 1755 the adjacent farms of Sallachary, Torrcruin, Carnoch, Achglyne and Sourlies hosted thirteen families and 78 people.

By 1841 they were reduced to eight families and 41 people, and most of this decline probably took place in 1764. Equally, Scottos became a sheep run from 1784, and by 1841 only supported eight people. In previous centuries it had been one of the most important estates in Knoydart. Our best guides to the old settlement pattern are probably the lists of placenames provided by the 1637 charter and by Father John Macdonald in Canada.

What we meet in the nineteenth century was already artificial. The total population was remarkably similar in 1841 to 1764, but it was distributed differently. The five neighbouring settlements of Neagart, Earar, Samadalan, Dun and Ridarrach now contained 488 people, or more than half of the whole population of Knoydart. (In terms of their Norse land-assessments the same places only accounted for about an eighth of Knoydart's total valuation.) This was a grossly imbalanced distribution pattern and must have developed between 1755 and 1841. The precise reasons elude us, but evictions from Scottos when it became a sheep run in 1784 were partly responsible. The Forfeited Estates Commissioners favoured 'improvement', but when this meant eviction from some farms it inevitably brought congestion to others.

Population Summary

The statistics we have for population and emigration are given in Figures 4 and 5. From these we can conclude that the total population had already reached about 1000 in 1764, and hovered near this mark between 1764 and 1853. At various stages between 2000 and 2500 people emigrated or were cleared off the land. The proportion of males was normally just under half. The figures from both Reverend Maciver and the nineteenth-century census returns suggest that half the population was under the age of twenty. Average household size was about five and it was normally the case that each family occupied one house. Short lives meant there were not many old to be supported and, in the case of large families, it appears from the census returns that some of the children were distributed amongst their relatives.

There are two separate questions to be answered here. Why was the population of Knoydart already so high in 1764, and why did it expand so rapidly for the next ninety years? In order to answer these we must address the issue of how a population expands. This is not a facetious question. The more one looks into it, the more contributory factors appear. At one level there are two simple reasons, either there are more births, or people live longer. If they live longer, there will in turn be more births. However, it seems unlikely that the birth rate in Knoydart varied greatly.

There are times, such as periods of great hardship, when a birth rate is depressed. Conversely, economic advantages, such as generous family allowances, have been known to enhance it. In 1755, half the population of Knoydart was under eighteen which means there was a high proportion of young women of child-bearing age. In 1841, the proportions are almost the same, which suggests that throughout Knoydart's history half its population was under twenty and just over half of these were female. These ratios are consistent and so, probably, was the birth rate. With such a high proportion of young women there was always the potential for rapid population growth. We can only assume that poverty, hunger and disease acted as effective checks throughout Knoydart's previous history.

The real motors of demographic change were lower infant mortality and longer lives. Food supply increased with potatoes and an increased stock of cattle. This took place well before the price rises of the Napoleonic wars. We do not know exactly when potatoes were introduced into Knoydart but they were certainly there by 1755–6 when Mungo Campbell reported them. It is unlikely they were, by themselves, responsible for an explosion in population between 1740 and 1764. Given the negative effects of manpower loss at Culloden, and the punishment expeditions thereafter, it appears likely that Knoydart's population had already approached 1000 early in the eighteenth century. Smallpox vaccination certainly began to have a dramatic effect throughout the Highlands later in the century, but in Knoydart's case this probably only applied after about 1770. In the same period, living conditions improved as creel huts were replaced by stone houses. In the nineteenth century men travelled from home to supplement their income with seasonal employment elsewhere. All of these are good reasons for population expansion after 1750, but they still do not answer the question of why population was already high.

In trying to address this issue we can assess some of the other causes that have been advanced for the population explosion. Bloody clan disputes are more persuasive as a check on population in the Middle Ages than the eighteenth century. Culloden probably had little lasting effect on the number of people in Knoydart, despite the loss of twenty-two men with Scottos. It is more likely that the removal of cattle in the punitive expeditions thereafter depressed the local economy for some years.

If population had already reached almost 1000 early in the eighteenth century, then both process and cause remain hidden from us. This is simply because of the absence of data. One piece of evidence that population pressure was causing severe economic and social problems in Skye, is provided by the infamous episode of the *Soitheach nan Daoine* in 1739. It appears that Sir Alexander Macdonald and one of the Macleods arranged for the forcible abduction, transportation and sale of a large number of their impoverished clansmen to North America. In the event they were shipwrecked off Ireland and the story leaked out. Coll Barrisdale's blackmail racket may have been partly a response to population pressure.

Knoydart's economy was always pastoral. The figures from Morison's survey of 1771 make it clear what a tiny proportion of land was arable as opposed to grazing. Between 1771 and 1853 it may be that there was a slight increase in the arable acreage of Knoydart, simply by virtue of population pressure to plant more potatoes in lazybeds; but in overall terms there can only ever have been a tiny percentage increase in the area of cultivated land. After 1853 these lazybeds collapsed into disuse again.

Given that Knoydart's economy was pastoral, but also given that until the general introduction of potatoes from the mid-eighteenth century the Highlander's staple was oatmeal, the next issue is the interdependence of the Knoydart economy with the outside world. We know from Mungo Campbell in 1755–6 that the people of Knoydart exchanged their butter and cheese for oatmeal with the people of Sleat, the garden of Skye. This is a good example of regional specialization. Geographically, there are differences between these two Highland areas and so each developed different functions – perhaps very early. Equally, it is possible that a trade in driven cattle may have existed for centuries. Historically, we associate the golden age of the droving trade with the eighteenth and nineteenth centuries but this may reflect our lack of information for earlier periods. In 1745, according to the Chevalier de Johnstone,

> there was great abundance of horned cattle, since their riches consisted of these, of which they sold a hundred thousand annually to the English.

The Chevalier's particular friend in the Highland ranks was Donald of Scottos, so possibly his remarks include some cattle from Knoydart. The area is remote but it is still on the mainland and there is no reason why surplus cattle should not be driven each year through the eastern passes to the Great Glen and beyond. Historically, the Knoydart people had much communication with their relations in Glengarry and also the Camerons, who were significantly involved in Knoydart during the sixteenth century. We do not have concrete evidence, but it is feasible that cattle were driven from Knoydart throughout the seventeenth century and perhaps earlier still. Certainly we have evidence of a similar cattle-trade from Argyll and the Southern Hebrides in the sixteenth and seventeenth centuries.

This is an important point because it prevents the assumption that Knoydart's economy existed in isolation until it was ground down on the anvil of capitalism from the mid-eighteenth century. What happens in the eighteenth century is that we witness the exposure of Knoydart's economy and people to the fluctuations of economic activity elsewhere. As economic interdependence between Highlands and Lowlands grew, so, paradoxically, did Knoydart's dependence. Its economic system was simple and inflexible. It lacked resilience and could not respond quickly to external circumstances. It had nothing on which to fall back, beyond its narrow agricultural base.

In the medieval period, when there was comparatively little trade with the Lowlands, there was less vulnerability to fluctuations in value. Bad seasons always adversely affected the Highlands. Either population was checked or the Highlanders stole from each other, the Lowlands, or the Irish. We do not know how cattle droving grew, but on the evidence of the Chevalier de Johnstone, it was thriving by 1745. A trade this size brought much needed cash to the Highland economy and afforded Highlanders the ability to buy the oatmeal they needed but which they could not grow in sufficient quantities themselves. It enabled them to maintain their population. However, the other side of the coin is that as this trade grew so did the High-landers' dependence on the outside world. Any slump in cattle prices materially affected large numbers of families by altering the terms of trade. This was already a factor by 1745. Conversely, any rise in prices, as during the Napoleonic wars, cushioned them.

The Chevalier's figure also helps us to gauge the negative economic effects of the aftermath of Culloden. We know that the punishment expeditions in 1747 carried off at least 20,000 head of livestock to Fort Augustus – over and above what they consumed in the field. We can assume that most of these were cattle from the Jacobite clans of the West Highland mainland, not from the islands and not from the Hanoverian clans of Argyll or the far North. The figure of 20,000 must represent a very high proportion of their stock. Certainly it meant no surplus for trade that year, and possibly for several years thereafter as herds were built up again. The punishment raids and the ending of large-scale cattle-reiving as practised by Coll of Barrisdale had as severe economic consequences as any loss on the battlefield.

Interdependence also created dependence. In a barter system, such as probably existed in early days, a cow would be reckoned in terms of so many bolls of meal. One of the complaints of the emigrants on the *Batchelor* in 1774 was that their cattle had halved in value in the previous few years. Not only had cattle decreased in value but corn had risen in price due to increased demand from distilleries. Ordinary Highland farmers had no control over this. Several emigrants on the *Batchelor* complained bitterly about the middlemen, the factors and drovers, who set the prices and so the terms of trade. What these fluctuations meant in practical terms for Highlanders was:

- When cattle prices rose, as they had done for several years before 1767, rents had been increased.
- Now that cattle prices were falling the rents were not falling with them.
- Corn prices had also risen.

In the balance between income and expenditure their income, which largely depended on cattle, had halved, whereas their expenditure on rents and corn had increased. Several emigrants pointed out that this meant ruin. If we add to these factors the effects of bad harvests (1772–4) and consequent cattle death then parts of the Highland economy simply could not absorb such stresses.

There is evidence from several areas that the early emigrations of the latter half of the eighteenth century consisted of people who had some means. This is borne out by the evidence of the *Batchelor*, where the migrants were often small farmers who had formerly employed others. If we apply this model to Knoydart it fits very well. Emigration in the period 1770–1800 creamed off the intermediate tenants, those who had some capital. Some, such as Spanish John, went on the *Pearl* in 1773, but there was an even more dramatic emigration in 1786 when a large number of tenants quit.

A contemporary, Bishop Alexander Macdonald, wrote of the damage this did to the Catholic Church:

> For those who emigrate, are just the people who are a little better off, and from whom the priest received hospitality whilst on his journeys. Those who remain, on the other hand, are mostly those who could not afford the cost of emigration, and are also quite unable to help the priest.

The emigration of such large numbers of small tenants affected the social structure for those left behind. Society tended to polarize between two extremes, those who owned the land and those who were crofters or cottars. The crofters, still less the cottars, had no capital to invest and could not raise themselves up the social or economic scale. At the same time a rising population always pressed for subdivision of land and resources. By the nineteenth century there were two strata in Knoydart, a large, depressed and impoverished tenantry below a distant or absentee landlord. The latter ruled through factors whose interests identified with the landowner rather than the tenants. So in 1883, Mr Baird, who had a firm resolve to let his large sheep-farms in smaller units to local tenants found that there simply were not any with the resources.

Reasons for Emigration.

Why did people emigrate – particularly in the eighteenth century? Our starting point is the evidence of Reverend Colin Maciver, Minister of Glenelg, in the Old Statistical Account of 1793:

> Emigration is thought to be owing in a great measure to the introduction of sheep, as one man often rents a farm where formerly many families lived comfortably; … But this is not solely the cause; the high rents demanded by landlords, the increase of population, and the flattering accounts received from their friends in America, do also contribute to the evil.

It is seldom we are given the reasons for particular families emigrating but in the period 1774–5 customs officials questioned those on board several ships and their summaries have survived. Of these the analysis of the *Batchelor* which carried some 131 passengers from Sutherland and Caithness to North Carolina is the most informative. The similarities between the rural economies of Sutherland and Knoydart allow us to draw parallels. Both were grazing countries, in both the farmers depended primarily on the income from their cattle, in both the people had to import their meal from elsewhere, and both are remote. Some reasons are particular to the families concerned, more of them are generally applicable throughout the Highland area.

The reasons fall into two types, positive and negative. The positive reasons are simply that the people of the Highlands received tremendous encouragement to go to America from friends and relations who had emigrated previously. Great prospects were held out for them, one day's wage would keep a man for a week, one man's wage would maintain a family of twenty. Land and provisions were cheap, whilst the price of labour was high. Tradesmen and artisans would find a market for their skills. No doubt such stories were seized upon by the naive and gullible, whilst the more sanguine consoled themselves that the situation could not possibly be worse than that they found at home. At the end of the day it must be admitted that the situation in the New World did hold out better prospects. Economic opportunity was always greater in North America than it was in the barren Highlands where landowners had a stranglehold on land and every other lever of economic power.

The negative reasons were equally strong. The evidence from the *Batchelor* paints a dismal picture. For a number of years both cattle prices and rents had risen. The problem for the people of Sutherland was that between 1767 and 1774 cattle prices had fallen by about 50%, whilst rents had either stayed the same or risen even further. Since most farmers depended primarily on cattle for their incomes there was now a yawning gap between income and expenditure. Against this backdrop of the general decline in cattle prices there were the particular circumstances of 1771–1774 when poor weather and bad harvests brought crop failure and high mortality to cattle stocks. 1772 was particularly acute. At the same time the price of grain had risen sharply, principally because of increased demand from the distilleries.

There is considerable debate among historians about the causes of the emigration from the Highlands. This is not just a matter of academic argument since it also informs attitudes to the issues of landownership and land-reform today. For some the reason was simply over-population, for others it was rent increases by greedy landowners. Throw in Jacobitism, political repression, the ending of the clan system, Cheviot sheep, deer-stalking and the social contrast between laird and crofter, and we have a volatile mix for the history-maker. The historian's job must always be to try and establish what *actually* caused emigration, despite the political arguments then and since.

We do not have detailed examinations of the reasons for emigration from Knoydart. However, Mr Maciver's comments in the Old Statistical Account bear out what we learn from Sutherland. Rents had risen and fluctuating cattle prices meant that pastoral districts like Knoydart were vulnerable since the tenants had no other means of boosting their incomes. At the same time, they were hearing very flattering accounts of the standards of living that could be achieved in North America. It was also more profitable for the landowner to let a sheep-farm to one man than to lots of small tenants.

We have some other pieces of evidence. In 1771, Morison argued that rent increases should not be too high on the Barrisdale estate. His comments imply that increased rents had already driven some from other parts of Knoydart:

> The Inhabitants of this estate in general have only Creel
> huts, and are at present far from being in opulent
> circumstances. I am humbly of Opinion that the
> additional rent proposed is as much as they can bear, at
> least for some years – to lay a high additional rent upon
> them all at once would certainly dispirit them, and tempt
> them either to grow desperate in the Country, or like their
> Neighbours to emigrate to America.

Fraser-Mackintosh has shown that the rental of Scottos estate
rose by nearly 700% between 1773 and 1795, whilst the number
of tenants reduced from twenty-seven to three. In addition to
the tenants there were a large number of dependent cottars and
it appears that most of both groups went to America in 1786
(*See* Figure 5). The rental of the whole Glengarry estate showed
a similar increase between 1768 and 1802. It is always difficult
assessing rent increases since these sometimes include the
commutation of services (i.e. that part of the rent that was
previously paid in kind or labour). However, the trend is clear.
There was no means by which a traditional tenant farmer could
cope with such an increase.

We also have contemporary evidence of population pressure.
Austin Macdonald, priest, wrote of Knoydart in 1787:

> The overpopulation of these districts, together with the
> oppression of the landlords are the principal causes of
> the departure of so many.

Today, many landowners in the Highlands have no clan
associations at all. Sometimes this is regretted and a certain
amount of historical nostalgia creeps into descriptions of the
old clan system. In fact, the hereditary chiefs were often ruthless
in their demands and expectations. Fraser-Mackintosh quotes a
letter from the young Glengarry in 1794, taking us past the
sentimentality of clan kinship to the true nature of Highland
landlordism. Glengarry is writing to his agent in Inverness:

> Enclosed you have a list of small tenants belonging to my
> Knoydart property – their leases being expired by
> Whitsunday first – and having refused to serve me, I have
> fully determined to warn them out, and turn them off my

property, without loss of time; and as this is the first order of the kind I have given you since I came of age, I have only to add that your punctuality and expedition on the present occasion will be marked by me.

There follows a list of twenty-nine tenants, from all round Knoydart, who had refused themselves, or members of their family, to Glengarry. The list ends on an ominous note:

Their cottars must be particularly specified, as they have a great number of them that refused.

The letter is written from Scamadale, just two months after Glengarry had turned twenty-one and taken control of his own affairs. He had been made a colonel, with power to raise a regiment. No doubt he was visiting his western estate to call out his men. The new chief dreamed of martial glory – and then his tenants refused to enlist! The pique and fury of a young man thwarted in his ambition is almost tangible. The reluctant tenants must be punished – and savagely. He was too impatient to even wait to get home before starting the process of revenge. Forced recruitment is an aspect of the clan system that has not received the attention it deserves. It existed even more strongly in earlier periods, and faced by such economic blackmail it is little wonder so many emigrated.

Can we give an overall rationale for emigration from Knoydart? As in every other part of the Highlands there is a welter of issues to be dealt with. Nevertheless we can detect general patterns because, as Marianne McLean has pointed out, emigration from Knoydart, particularly in 1786, took on the nature of a communal response to an overwhelming economic problem.

Despite emigration, Knoydart's population remained about 1000 from perhaps the early eighteenth century until 1853. There was a fundamental disjunction between the growing numbers of people, the resources available to them, and the wealth they could create in a poor agricultural environment. Against a background of rising expectations this would inevitably lead to emigration, simply for economic betterment. There is no doubt many did leave Knoydart for precisely these reasons, particularly in 1773 and 1786. The trigger may have been bad harvests and rent rises, but these tenants could foresee the general economic trend and decided to go whilst they could. To an extent, they were what we would call economic migrants. The people of Knoydart were squeezed between a barren environment, their own increasing numbers, general economic patterns, rising expectations and the unchecked power of their landowner.

The causes of particular emigrations were rent rises and the eviction of small tenants in favour of sheepfarmers. The reasons for, and pace of, this transformation were partly set by prevailing economic circumstances and partly by the greed, selfishness and level of indebtedness of the landowners. The Clearance of 1853 was the last spasm in a conflict which occurred because landowner and tenant no longer shared economic or social interests.

Chapter 9

THE 1853 CLEARANCE

All accounts of the Knoydart evictions begin and end with Donald Ross. In 1853 the area was the scene of one of the last great clearances in Scotland. Ross, a Glasgow advocate, was so incensed by the cruelty that he travelled to Knoydart, interviewed those who remained and wrote a passionate little book called *The Glengarry Evictions*. It is not very long, just thirty-one pages, but in it he gives a harrowing account of the events of that summer and autumn in Knoydart. Despite objective arguments about the inevitability of depopulation, of the inescapable disjunction between resources and expectations, this little book is enough to make anyone's blood boil. In its pages Ross gives a general account of events and a series of case-histories. His arguments, although impassioned, are remarkably temperate. A deeply moral man and a strong Christian, his humanity was appalled at what he saw in Knoydart. His motives, as those of Coll Macdonald, the Catholic priest at Sandaig who tried to shelter those evicted, were wholly admirable.

He gives report after report on the families who suffered, every one different, but each the same in its essential features. He was horrified at the cruelty and brutality, the callousness of a system that would allow such abuse of power; and he did his best to alleviate some of the distress with practical help. It is a very humane book and a welcome antidote to the objectivity every historian tries to adopt. Today it would be called photo-journalism, and as a simple straightforward account of the miseries involved in Clearance it is unequalled. We cannot criticise his humanity, even if we question his premises, challenge some of his proposals, and suggest that he did not follow his arguments through to their logical conclusion.

Nevertheless, at a distance of 150 years we must try to look beyond the harrowing images to establish the facts, the patterns, the truth; aspects which overmuch emotional investment can blur or block out. There is no doubt that Donald Ross gives a broadly accurate picture of what happened. There are a few errors and inaccuracies in his account, and doubtless some exaggeration. His partisan approach encouraged him to understate contrary arguments or facts, to uncritically accept certain statements or opinions. Despite this the following are generally true:

- On 9 August 1853 some 332 people were taken to Canada aboard the *Sillery*.
- Towards the end of the same month, at least another sixty-one were made homeless by forcible eviction and the demolition of their houses.
- At the same time, at least another thirty-four were threatened with eviction and the destruction of their homes. In most cases it was sickness that prevented this taking place immediately.
- Those who were evicted tried to erect temporary shelters, from which they were repeatedly driven away and the shelters destroyed. This happened up to six times.
- The other residents of Knoydart were warned and threatened against taking in any of the evicted families.
- Some of the evictions were probably motivated by a desire to prevent old and uneconomic residents from remaining on the estate and eventually claiming poor relief.

The general background is given by Ross in the following terms:

Last spring all the crofters on the Glengarry estates in Knoydart were served with summonses of removal, accompanied with a verbal message from Mrs. McDonell and her factor that Sir John McNeil, chairman of the Board of Supervision, Edinburgh, had agreed to convey them all to Australia ... The poor people had no alternative but to accept of any offer that might be made to them ... Shortly after this, another intimation reached the tenants, viz: that their destination was North America, that a ship would be at 'Isle Oronsay' in Skye, in a short time to receive them, and that they must go on board ... Some families refused to go to Canada, ... and these, along with some others, for whom there was no room on board, are still in Knoydart.

After ... Mrs McDonell's factor, an old gentleman by the name of Grant, returned to Knoydart and commenced the work of destruction on the houses of the crofters and cottars. Not only the houses of those who had left the country, but also the houses of those who refused to go, were pulled to the ground ... The few huts left standing are occupied by paupers who are on the poors' roll of the parish, but the factor before leaving the district warned these poor creatures that if they allowed any one of the evicted people shelter, for one moment ... that he would cause their huts immediately thereafter to be levelled to the ground ...

Eleven families, comprising upwards of sixty individuals, were on this night with no other shelter in Knoydart.

Knoydart belonged to the Macdonells of Glengarry and, during the first half of the nineteenth century, this family was desperately troubled by debt. After the chief died in 1852 his widow and the trustees for his young son prepared to sell the estate. A successful sale to a sheepfarmer was more likely if the tenants were evicted. It is a familiar story in the Highlands, – a once-great family living beyond their means; sustained by an inflated view of their own self-importance, status and position; supported by their dependants in this cultural myopia. From a cost-conscious and democratic age we lack sympathy for such an outlook but must recognise that they were creatures of the society from which they came. What such attitudes meant for the ordinary occupants of Knoydart is shown in Ross's interviews with those who were left behind.

John McKinnon, a cottar, aged 44, is married, and has a wife and six children … When McKinnon's house was pulled down he had no place to put his head in; consequently himself and his family for the first night or two, had to burrow among the rocks near the shore … McKinnon's wife was pregnant when she was turned out of her house among the rocks. In about four days thereafter she had a premature birth; and this and the exposure to the elements, and the want of proper shelter and a nutritious diet, has brought on consumption, from which there is no chance whatever of her recovery.

Charles McDonald, aged 70 years, is a widower and has no family … When the factor and his party arrived at Charles's door they knocked and … ordered the old man to quit – 'As soon as I can,' said Charles, and, taking up his plaid and staff and adjusting his blue bonnet, he walked out … Charles took to the rocks, and from that day to this he has never gone near his old habitation. He has no house nor home, but receives occasional supplies of food from his evicted neighbours, and he sleeps on the hill!

Alexander McDonald, aged 40 years. Has a wife and family … Alexander's house was also pulled down. His wife was pregnant, still the levellers thrust her out, and then put the children out after her. The husband argued … but it was all in vain, for in a few minutes all he had for his … home was a lot of rubbish, blackened rafters and heaps of stones. The levellers laughed at him and his protests … Alexander, had, like the rest of his evicted brethren, to burrow among the rocks and in caves until he put up a temporary shelter amid the wreck of his old habitation, but from which he was repeatedly driven away. For three days Alexander McDonald's wife lay sick beside a bush, where, owing to terror and exposure to cold, etc. she had a miscarriage. She was then removed to the shelter of the walls of her former house, and for three days she lay so ill that her life was despaired of.

In the face of such abuse the question immediately occurs as to why there was no physical resistance. Ross tacitly asks and answers this question himself when describing the destruction of the home of Allan MacDonald, aged fifty-four, a widower with four children.

> The indignation of Allan, however, was frequently roused owing to the treatment he had received, and, he said, that had it not been for his poor children, who had so long looked up to him for protection and support, that he would have resisted the doings of the factor to the last inch of his existence. And Allan could do it. He was a strong, well-made highlander, and well able to show determined resistance in any case of invasion.

Allan, though, had four children to care for, including a twelve-year-old boy suffering from severe colic. In the light of the possible consequences, resistance was irresponsible and so he had to swallow his anger for the sake of his family.

Ross makes a number of points, some of which are incontrovertible, with regard to the cruelty of the evictions.

- There is no doubt that the people were just regarded as encumbrances to be disposed of, first of all to Australia, then Canada. Allan, for instance, would have gone to Australia, where he already had two children, but not to Canada.
- In the case of the elderly, emigration was not an option. Elizabeth Gillies (60) and Charles Macdonald (70) had no family. How on earth were they to maintain themselves in the New World?
- In some cases there was a natural unwillingness to take passage whilst members of the family were seriously ill.
- The landowner trod heavily on the rights of those evicted. In practical terms the victims had no means of legal redress because of their poverty, ignorance and remoteness.
- One landless family willing to emigrate to America was denied free passage with the claim that there was no room on the boat. They were still evicted.

What happened was unforgivable. But, over and beyond every act of cruelty, we are still left with fundamental dilemmas which Donald Ross, in his compassion, did not address. His premise was that people implied agricultural improvement. He believed that crofters could profitably cultivate the land.

> The land is adapted for a crofter population; and, had the proprietor and factor encouraged the crofters by leases and otherwise, they might have got them to raise from the soil excellent crops of potatoes, turnips and vegetables, together with some corn, and this, with the produce of the fishing, and the sale of sheep and cattle, they might not only have paid their rents, but have plenty for their own support. There was no encouragement however given to the crofters to improve, no motive held out for exertion; sheep farms were closing in upon them upon the right and upon the left; ... The soil of Knoydart is good, and, as already stated, had the crofters got leases, that is, security of tenure for 19 or 27 years, they might have built good houses, brought into cultivation much land, and have lived comfortably, and paid rents regularly.

Ross shared, along with the factors of the Forfeited Estates nearly a century earlier, an almost axiomatic belief in the virtues of improvement. Grant long leases, give opportunity and the enterprise of man would do the rest. This naive optimism, conceived in more fertile regions of Britain, could not withstand the winds and rain of the long Highland winter. From our perspective in the late twentieth century, with hill-farms so dependent on government subsidy, we can see the inevitability of decline. Against more fertile soils in kinder climes, farming in the barren hills of Knoydart is at a fatal disadvantage. Despite the failure of the potato crop in 1846, despite the poverty and desperation of the preceding eighty years, Donald Ross still believed that agriculture could sustain a population in Knoydart. In this, he, along with many before and since, was probably wrong.

There is an almost Biblical quality to his beliefs. His starting-point was that man had a duty to tame nature by means of agriculture:

when a whole country-side is at one fell swoop cleared of
its population to make room for sheep, … when the march
of improvement and cultivation is checked, and when the
country is transformed into a wilderness and the land to
perpetual barrenness, not only are the best feelings of our
common humanity violated, but the decree is tantamount
to interdicting the command of the Most High who said
to man, 'Go, replenish the earth, and subdue it.'

Ross was not prepared to carry his arguments through to their
logical conclusion. He did not directly attack the property rights
of landowners.

I can understand well how a landlord at times may have
to resort to a judicious weeding – how to extend crofts he
may occasionally have to remove refractory or useless
tenants from one district to another

but at the same time Ross argued for the rights of the indigenous
population

without at all questioning the rights of property, these
highland men and highland women have as much right
to remain in old Scotland as the higher and middle classes
have.

But this is the crux of the matter, and a dilemma which Donald
Ross and many others have never faced. When these two 'rights'
come into conflict they are fundamentally irreconcilable. For
Knoydart's men and women to have remained would have
constituted an assault on what were then understood to be the
rights of property. Donald Ross did not attack these in principle,
he merely complained about the manner and practice of the
evictions. He did not hold that property rights were themselves
immoral, but that this particular eviction was accompanied by
unChristian conduct.

Some mercy should be shown to the unfortunate beings
who were to be removed; the clearance should be carried
through at a proper season, and with as much respect to
the feelings as well as to the persons of the parties removed
as possible.

Ross was not alone in commenting on the Knoydart Clearances. A number of newspapers covered the event, particularly the fate of those who did not go to Canada. Many felt the landlord was simply trying to evict those who might become paupers and so the issue widened to include attacks on the administration of the poor law in Scotland. During the subsequent debate, particular differences emerged and the arguments over detail can obscure the central themes. Let us leave to one side the issues of just how much the crofters owed in arrears, how much the landlord contributed in the way of emigration costs, how well the poor relief system worked in Glenelg compared to other parts of contemporary Scotland. There remain some fundamental questions. What were the motives of the landowner? What were the respective rights of landowner and tenant? Could crofting in Knoydart ever be profitable?

Despite attempts to defend Mrs Macdonell and the other trustees of the Glengarry Estate their motives do not bear scrutiny. The cruelty of the eviction, the repeated destruction of the temporary shelters of those evicted, the offers of free transport out of the district, all demonstrate the private agenda of the landowner. Poor tenants were to be got rid of – regardless. In time this would increase the value of the property, make it easier to sell, and reduce the burden of maintaining paupers. The benefits for the landowner were obvious and tangible. The supposed benefits for the evicted were simply ugly rationalisations. It was not concern for them that was the reason for eviction and, in the case of the old or the sick, clearance was especially callous. With hindsight we can agree that the tenants were better off elsewhere but such motives, whether in Knoydart or dozens of other clearances, are unacceptable from a democratic viewpoint. The fact that in the long-term the people prospered in the New World is irrelevant to the issue of whether they were wronged in the Highlands. They were turned out of their homes and stripped of their lands, the industry of generations. Thanks to the landlord they were left with no capital except their labour.

The question of rights was less relevant from a contemporary perspective than from ours. Whatever their moral right, legally

Knoydart – Population Distribution 1851

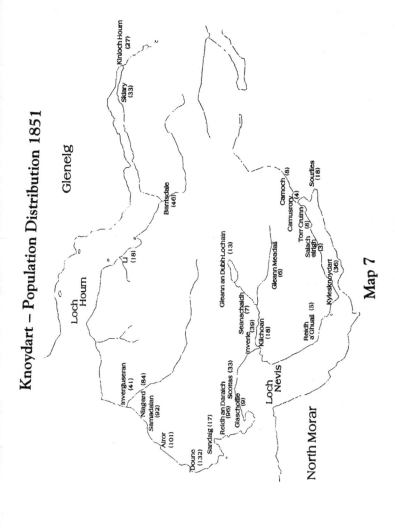

Glenelg

Loch Houm

Kinloch Houm (27)

Skiary (33)

Barrisdale (46)

Li (18)

Gleann an Dubh-Lochain (13)

Inverguseran (41)

Niagard (84)

Samadalan (92)

Airor (101)

Doune (132)

Sandaig (17)

Reidh an Daraich (96)

Scottas (33)

Glaschoille (9)

Seanachaidh (7)

Inverie (39)

Kilchoan (18)

Gleann Meadail (6)

Carnoch (8)

Camusrory (4)

Torr Cruinn (8)

Salach aridh (3)

Sourlies (18)

Reidh a Ghuail (5)

Kylesknoydart (36)

Loch Nevis

North Morar

Map 7

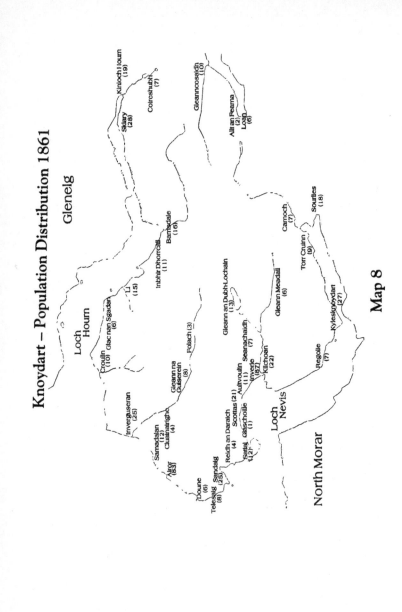

Knoydart – Population Distribution 1861

Glenelg

Loch Hourn

Kinlochhourn (19)
Skiary (28)
Coireshubh (7)
Gleanncosaidh (10)
Allt an Peama (2)
Loan (6)

Li (15)
Barrisdale (16)
Inbhir Dhorrcail (11)

Croulin (10)
Glac nan Sgadan (6)
Inverguseran (25)
Gleann na Guiserein (8)
Folach (3)

Samadalan (12)
Cluainairigh (4)
Airor (83)
Doune (6)
Sandaig (25)
Teleralg (8)
Reidh an Daraich (4)
Scottas (21)
Sallad Gàschoille (12)
Gàschoille (1)

Gleann an Dubh-Lochain (13)
Aulfvoulin (11)
Inverie (687)
Seenachaidh (7)
Kilchoan (22)

Gleann Meadail (6)
Carnoch (7)
Torr Crúinn (9)
Sourlies (18)

Regolle (7)
Kyleskinoydart (27)

Loch Nevis

North Morar

Map 8

the tenants had no chance of withstanding landlord power in Scotland in 1853. The question of landlord motives was not then subject to the sort of democratic challenge we might raise today. However, as was demonstrated as recently as 1948, the legal position of landowners remains unassailed. The fact that land reform has made little progress in 150 years is one of the reasons the clearances are still so topical today.

One of the central points of debate, then and now, is the question of economic alternatives. Between the mid-eighteenth century and 1948, one argument against clearance was that somehow agriculture could be made to work if it was properly, differently, organised. Taking the longer view it is plain that in areas like Knoydart, agriculture has always been doomed. Seen from the perspective of the late twentieth century an agricultural base for the Highland economy becomes more unlikely with each generation. There is an unpleasant irony to this since effectively we have to concede that in economic terms the crofter could not compete with the sheep farm or the deer forest, that there was an historic inevitability about rural depopulation in the Highlands, whether resulting from clearance or emigration, and that the lairds were simply catching the economic tide. This leaves us burdened with the dilemma that whilst landlords are wrong, the landlords were right.

Retrospective

Notwithstanding the condemnation of future generations, the evictions represented a triumph for the landowners. They had secured what they wanted, an empty estate. We can only guess at the psychological effects of the clearance on the rest of the population of Knoydart. It must have represented a major trauma, and reinforced despair at the overwhelming rights of property as recognised by the British state. Despite a public outcry the landlord had gained a complete victory. It appeared later that some of those evicted had managed, by sheer tenacity, to remain in Knoydart. But others among the weak and old fell prematurely by the wayside.

The cold facts of the clearance are best illustrated by comparing the census returns for 1851 and 1861 (See Maps 7 and 8). There is a common misapprehension that the entire population was cleared. This is not so. Even after the evictions there remained nearly 600 people in Knoydart in 1861. We also have some valuable first-hand evidence from Gillies MacIsaac, whose family was evicted in 1853 when he was a boy of twelve. In July 1894 he gave evidence before the Deer Forest Commission sitting at Inverie.

Gillies MacKissock (aged fifty-four)

Where is the nearest crofting township? – *Rhidarroch….*

Are there crofters there just now? – *No, not one.*

Was it an old crofting township? – *Yes.*

Do you know how many crofters were there? – *I think seven or eight.*

Can you tell us of any other crofting township on the property? – *Yes; Dune was another crofting township.*

How many crofters were there? – *Fourteen or fifteen.*

When was that latter place cleared? – *About forty-one years ago.*

And when were they removed from Rhidarroch? – *The same year.*

Where were they removed to? – *To America.*

They were cleared off the estate? – *Yes, they were summoned off the land.*

Did they get any assistance to emigrate? – *Yes, they got their passage paid.*

Did they leave this country of their own accord, or were they evicted? – *They were evicted.*

Are there not descendants of these people still on the estate? – *A few of them; I am one of them myself....*

Can you tell us of any other available land besides the two places you have named? – *The next township is called Airor; it is occupied by crofters at present. The next township is Samadalan.*

Are there any crofters there now? – *Not one, only a shepherd.*

How is the land occupied? – *It is under sheep and deer.*

To whom do they belong? – *To the proprietor.*

How many crofters were there formerly? – *Thirteen or fourteen, I fancy.*

When was it cleared? – *At the same time, – about forty-one years ago.*

Did the former residents in that township go to America also? – *They were evicted, 332 persons. ...*

Do you know anything about the circumstances in which the people were who occupied these crofting townships? – *They were crofters and fishermen combined. ...*

Did any of them remain in this place itself after they were put out of their holdings? – *Yes, they stopped on the estate in spite of them. I am a member of one of the families that stopped on the estate in spite of the proprietor or the proprietrix.*

How was that done? – *They managed it for four months, I may say, sleeping out under the shelter of walls and gardens and one place or another; because if they put up any sort of a house, no matter how small or of what shape, it would be broken down in three or four days' time. So from the middle of July of that year until about the middle of November they were living in that state. Then they got a sort of relief in the shape of tents, which they used for three years.*

Who provided these tents for them? – *The people of Glasgow and Edinburgh, I fancy, sent them home; and then again they would not be allowed to put them up in any place on the estate, but only on a small bit of ground that was attached to the Catholic Chapel at Sandaig.*

Did some of them put up a sort of shelter for themselves below high water-mark? – *Yes, they always kept near the places where they had had the crofts and houses; taking shelter about the walls of the houses they had in the best way they could.*

So that the evictions were attended by a great deal of cruelty and suffering? – *Yes. It was so hard that some days they could not get up a spark of fire to cook a bit of meat of any sort, and they had to do without anything to eat that day.*

And do you know the occasion of their removal? Why was it that they were removed? – *For the rich farmer who wanted to get the land.*

Then, it was to make way for the sheep farmer that they were removed? – *That was the reason, so far as I know....*

At the time of the evictions you would be about twelve years of age? – *About that.*

The districts that were cleared had become grossly overcrowded by 1853. In 1851, the coastal strip between the Guseran and Sandaig supported half the population of Knoydart. This was not justifiable on agricultural grounds and presumably derived from estate policy at the beginning of the nineteenth century. Apparently some immigration from Skye was permitted about 1835 which can only have compounded the population problem.

William MacInnes, Crofter, Airor (aged sixty-four)

Your people were not originally from Knoydart? – *No.*

Your father came, I think, from Skye? – *Yes.*

And all the crofters in Airor with one exception came from Skye about the same time? – *Yes, the parents of the present crofters.*

And they all settled there about the time of the evictions? – *They came there before the tenants were removed from Knoydart.*

The problem was that in the event of any economic downturn, such as failure of the potatoes or herring, these families of crofters and fishermen were dangerously exposed. Their vulnerability was compounded by a complete change in the attitude of the landowners. People were no longer a military, and therefore an economic, asset; they were now regarded as a liability.

History quickly becomes myth, especially where there is a strong emotional or moral investment. When discussing the Knoydart Clearances we must remember the economic background and changing demographic patterns. In a period of burgeoning expectations, the status quo was not an option. A microeconomic system that had worked, after a fashion, for thousands of years was simply ground to pieces during a period of enormous economic change. It happened recently enough for us to know something of the human misery involved, as families tried or failed to adjust to new circumstances. In many parts of the world it is happening still.

At the same time we should not let unpleasant facts escape us. The structures of power in Highland society were such that the burden of change was never borne equally. This factor still has relevance today because the issue of land ownership has never been resolved. Enormous areas of land are still in the hands of tiny numbers of people. Landowners or their agents were, are, quick to put their own construction on the past.

William MacKay, Solicitor, Inverness, Agent for Mr Bowlby (Proprietor)

Have you any reason to doubt the evidence given by the first witness as to the number of people who were at one time located on the estate as crofters? – *I should very much doubt that there were 330 persons removed....*

Don't you think there is old arable there? [Glendulochan] – *It is cultivated.*

All the old arable? – *Yes. Of course, you will find old 'lazy-beds' on the hill sides, but I should say it is centuries since they were used.*

Within two generations history was being rewritten, this time by the landowner's agent. The census evidence points to the figure of 332 being about right, and the lazybeds were probably cultivated in the period of maximum population growth between 1770 and 1841.

We can retell the story of the Clearances to every generation, but they are just another grievous example of the difficulties people have in adjusting to economic fundamentals. These were especially acute in a society so hierarchical and so ill-led, and for a people so legally subordinate. We cannot bring back the past, and there is no point in trying to. Equally we should not forget an evil done. William MacInnes, a crofter from Airor, said as much when giving evidence in 1894. He was answering the questions of Mr William MacKay, the landowner's agent.

Do you remember how many crofters were on Samadlan? – *No.*

Have you any idea? – *I think there were about twelve.*

Do you want them to come back again to the same holdings? – *Those who were there would not come home, supposing I sent for them; they are now in a home where they have no need of a croft.*

Knoydart – Population Distribution 1891

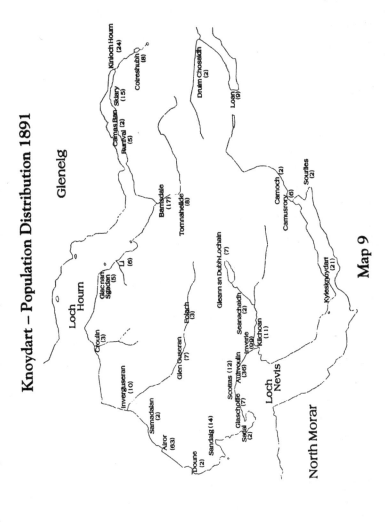

Glenelg

Loch Hourn

Kinloch Hourm (24)
Sklary (15)
Camas Ban (2)
Coireshubh (8)
Runival (5)

Druim Chosaidh (2)
Loan (9)

Barrisdale (17)
Tomnahalde (8)

Glac nan Sgadan (5)
(6)

Carnoch (2)
Camusrory (6)
Sourlies (2)

Cloulin (3)

Gleann an Dubh-Lochain (7)

Folach (3)

Glen Guseran (7)

Inverguseran (10)

Kylesknoydart (21)

Samadalan (2)

Scottas (12)
Airdvoulin (36)
Seanachaidh (2)
Inverie (99)
Kilchoan (11)

Glaschoille (7)
Sadal (2)

Loch Nevis

Airror (63)

Doune (2)

Sandaig (14)

North Morar

Map 9

Chapter 10

FROM 1853 TO 1891

Sources

We have official documents which provide rich sources of evidence for this period and allow us to fill in some detail for Knoydart. There was considerable pressure for land reform in the Highlands during the late nineteenth century. This resulted in two royal commissions – the Napier Commission and the Deer Forest Commission. Mr Baird, then owner of Knoydart, gave evidence before the Napier Commission in 1883, whilst the Deer Forest Commission, though less well-known, provides us with some particularly revealing evidence in 1894. We also have the six decennial census returns from 1841 to 1891 which we can use to draw maps showing demographic shifts (*See* Maps 7–9) and employment patterns. (*See* Figures 6 and 7).

From sheep to deer

The second half of the nineteenth century saw the continued erosion of traditional economic forms. Crofting could not sustain the population of Knoydart and sheep-farming, which had swept all before it for the best part of a century, went through a period of crisis. The landowners had preferred sheep to people and, undoubtedly, this worked to their economic advantage from about 1790 to about 1876. However sheep farming then became much less profitable and so most of Knoydart, along with huge swathes of the Highland landscape elsewhere, was converted from sheep farms to deer forest. Unfortunately, deer forests required even less human labour to maintain them and the social effect of this economic change was to create an ever more dependent population.

Hunting had always been regarded as an aristocratic pursuit and it drew visitors to the Highlands from the very beginning of the nineteenth century. Leyden, writing in 1800, says

> MacDonell of Glengary has constructed, on the side of Loch Nevis a little above Scothouse, a wicker house in the ancient manner, to serve as a hunting-box. The form of the house and the position of the rafters seem to be exactly imitated, and there is no ceiling but the roof. Instead, however, of forming the exterior walls with turf and sods, they have injudiciously covered it with slates – an excellent idea for a virtuoso and antiquary.

By the late Victorian period, hunting had become a craze. Sporting estates and shooting lodges were created all over the Highlands. Shooting and fishing parties came up from the South, occupied the big houses over the summer, employed locals, entertained, and left some money behind before departing again as winter approached. Sporting pursuits were not new, but their economic significance was now of a different order. As sheep farming became markedly less profitable, so large capital sums were invested in fencing deer forests. Shepherds became redundant, although some locals found employment as ghillies and stalkers.

The new industrial and commercial plutocrats could indulge their passions in less favoured parts of the Empire. For some it was big game in Africa, for others it was deer-stalking in Scotland. For Mr John Baird it was both. In a magazine article in 1886 a sketch was given of Mr Baird MP, who had recently inherited Knoydart from his uncle. It describes how he

> spent two winters in the Soudan, when he and Colonel Knox accounted for any amount of big game – elephants, lions, rhinoceroses, hippopotami, etc. ... Mr Baird killed an elephant within six weeks of his leaving England, which is tolerably sharp work.

Under the Bairds, the Bowlbys and the Brockets, Knoydart was developed as a shooting estate. Such an approach is less favoured today and it would be difficult to maintain that it was for the long-term economic benefit of the local population. In the light of the failure of the land raid in 1948, some were inclined to hark back to the halcyon days before Brocket. In objective terms the population fell from 412 in 1891 to about 80 in 1947, a decline which it would be harsh to attribute solely to Brocket, who only had the estate from the 1930s.

Quite apart from shooting and fishing there was an increasing interest in the Highlands as a tourist destination. To the modern eye the landscape is beautiful, but this view has itself a history to it. The beauty of the Highlands has to a great extent been invented, it was not always apparent to earlier visitors. In September 1746 one of Cumberland's army described the races staged at Fort Augustus for the entertainment of the troops. Both men and women participated and some contemporaries were rather scandalized at the proceedings. The author gives a quaint justification:

> It was necessary to entertain Life in this Manner; otherwise, by the constant View of Mountains surrounding us, we should have been affected with hypochondriacal Melancholy.

Similarly, the Census Enumerator in 1841 wrote of the area between Inverguseran and Inverie

> The whole District is poor, wet and dreary in the extreme.

On the other hand, in 1784 Ranald Macdonell of Scottos wrote, inviting the wife of a friend in Inverness to visit Scottos for her health

> did she reap no other benefit than the convenience of the sea bath, which is the best strengthener of the nerves yet known, and agrees with most constitutions.

Ranald must have been about sixty years old when he wrote this letter and as a military man we can assume he indulged in sea-bathing himself - though whether the waters of Loch Nevis strengthen or numb the nerves remains debatable.

The early nineteenth century also saw the emergence of an extraordinary fetish with real or imagined Celticisms; a trend which Glengarry, then owner of Knoydart, lived out to an extravagant degree.

> The only mansion-house in the parish, is that of Inverie, on Glengarry's Knodyart property, where he now resides. It is beautifully situated on the banks of Lochnevis, and was built by the late Colonel Macdonell, father of the present proprietor, who has been described as the last of that class of Highland Chiefs, of whom he formed so perfect a specimen in all his feelings and habits. The house is remarkable, inasmuch as the two principal rooms are finished with strong wattle work from the floor to the roof-tree, for there is no cieling. The couples which support the fabric are of native fir, of great strength and size, also rising from the ground and meeting in massive arches over-head. The floor is of clay and hard sand, the whole finishing being truly Celtic, and in excellent keeping with the tartans which grace its hospitable and accomplished inmates.
>
> (Reverend A. Beith, Minister of Glenelg, 1836)

Unfortunately this passion for maintaining the style of what he imagined was a true Highland chief proved ruinously expensive. It was as a direct result of the indebtedness of the Glengarry family that Knoydart was cleared and sold in the 1850s.

The evidence from the Napier and Deer Forest Commissions

In the last decades of the nineteenth century sheep farming, which had been the mainstay of the estate economy for a century, went through a period of crisis. This comes out clearly in the evidence Mr John Baird gave before the Napier Commission in 1883. Mr Baird professed a laudable desire to end the system of letting large sheep-farms to non-resident farmers. However, the middling ranks of local tenants had gone to America a century before and none of the crofters had the capital to take on such leases themselves. As a result the slump in wool and sheep prices meant that the farms fell back into his own hands. After losing money for several years simple economics dictated that he convert his sheep grazings into deer forest.

John Baird, at Portree, 1883

Can you give us any idea as to the causes which render the taking of these sheep farms so difficult to arrange, and also to what you attribute your own losses on the farms you occupy ? – *In the first place, the chief cause why these farms are not let is because I declined to let them on the same terms on which they were let before. I declined to let them to non-resident south country farmers. I wish to divide them so far as I can into sizes which would form respectable farms for respectable resident tenants, and hitherto I have not had offers for that class of farm that were at all acceptable....*

But it was not from a desire to convert the land into a deer forest, but really from inability to let it otherwise? – *If the land had been profitable to me, I should not have turned it into a deer forest....*

(*Of the crofters*) They could not very well leap up from their present holdings to a farm? – *I don't think any of them could.*

Mr Baird's statements also provide evidence of systematic overgrazing by the sheep-farmers. Of course the land was not theirs, they merely leased it, but with hindsight this exploitative policy may have done untold damage to the local environment. Sheep, like goats, wreak havoc when overstocked.

Have you any idea, from what you have heard from people formerly connected with sheep farming, what the cost of wintering sheep used to be in old days? – *So far as I know, there was less sending away of sheep in old days, and that was got at by there being few sheep on the place. In those days they kept only the number of sheep the land could winter and now, so far as I can make out, the number kept is the number the land can summer.*

Further evidence comes from the statements made by Mr William Mackay (Solicitor), agent for Mr. Bowlby (Proprietor), before the Deer Forest Commission in 1894. He revealed that in the previous decade nearly 70% of Knoydart had become deer forest.

How long is it since the sheep were removed to make way for the deer? – *The first land afforested was, I understand, Barrisdale, and the sheep were cleared about the year 1884 or 1885, when Mr. Baird was the proprietor. Then the upper portions of Scotas were cleared about 1890 or 1891. Then again last year Mr. Baird took a slice off Kilchoan and a slice off Inverguseran and enclosed the whole. … I know that in a certain case I altogether failed to let a deer forest in which there were sheep. Sportsmen will not look at a forest where there are sheep.*

Mr Mackay mounted a vigorous defence of his proprietor but it is apparent that there was a complete lack of understanding on the part of the estate of its crucial role in the local economy. There was no sense of responsibility for the predicament of dependent tenants. Estate work was only available as and when the estate chose to provide it. If there was no shooting for a year then local men would have to find something else to do. A sense of bitterness and alienation is present in some of the evidence, particularly from the youngest crofter spokesman.

Gillies MacKissock (aged fifty-four)

What is the usual occupation of the men here? – *As a rule they work for the proprietor.*

At ordinary estate work? – *Yes, now and again when they get it.*

And how do they manage to make a living otherwise? – *They plant a few barrels of potatoes.*

And do they maintain themselves partly by fishing? – *It is very little fishing they do….*

Are they paid for that [gamekeeping] by the year, or are they only paid for the time their services are required? – *While their services are required....*

Can you let me have any idea of the number of shepherds who were removed? – *... I should say five or six were removed.*

Since when? – *Since three years ago. There were twenty shepherds removed altogether.*

And you think that the stock is being diminished in order to make way for deer? – *I believe so. The stock has been reduced from 30,000 to less than 4000 sheep.*

William Macinnes, Crofter, Airor (aged sixty-four)

The crofters on Airor are very well off, are they not? – *Yes, but how?* – *They go far and near, and even abroad, to earn money for the families they leave at home. It is not the crofts at Airor that maintain the people.*

Don't you think it is better for them to do so than to remain at home even upon larger crofts? – *I think they could not stop at home yet, even if they had bigger crofts: it would not do.*

Some of them have built slated houses? – *Yes, but if so, it was not by means of the produce of the crofts....*

How many new houses have been put up at Airor? – *Two.*

And have these been put up by the earnings of the crofters' families in the south? – *Yes.*

Jonathan Macinnes, Crofter, Airor (aged thirty-one)

Do the crofters or their sons get employment in the forest? – *No ... I don't think they would give the chance of employment to any from the district if they could avoid it. ... I am quite sure I will not, if they can get it elsewhere ... They would be very sorry to give us any chance of employment … Ever since we applied to the Crofters Commission they have turned against us as much as they could.*

Mr Mackay was the last to speak to the Deer Forest Commission on the subject of Knoydart. Although an effective apologist for the landlord, he comes across as a rather unsympathetic character. Despite this, his hard-nosed realism is as relevant now as it was then.

Do you think the crofts there are of a sufficient size at present? – *Well, I think they are, in the circumstances, for this reason, that you cannot make crofts at Airor or anywhere on this estate sufficiently large to maintain a family.*

Why not? - *Because there is no ground. For example, on the whole of Samadalan there is only an area of about ten acres of what is known as old arable land. The bulk of that is not really worth turning over.…*

Now, do you agree with the evidence we have heard that a part of this estate is suitable for crofters' holdings? – *No. I went over the whole estate; and, in my opinion, – of course, you can take my view for what it is worth, but I cannot spot a single place where you can put down a crofting township with any degree of comfort at all.…*

Do you think the present condition of the land is less favourable to its occupation by a population of that number than it was when they were removed? – *I think so, and for this reason, that crofters are not now satisfied with living in the same way in which their forefathers lived forty or fifty years ago. … I believe it is the case with this estate … that we could not do better for the people than we are doing. Many of the cottars get employment on the estate, and I think that is better for them than if they had crofts, from which they would find it difficult to extract a livelihood.…*

Is it your opinion that it is the best use to put the land of Knoydart to, under deer? – *Yes, it is. … I know it did support sheep, and I know that for the last ten years there has been an enormous loss on the sheep farms.…*

And they made a living off it [the land]? – *They made a wretched living....*

That is not the traditionary account? – *Tradition paints the past in beautiful colours; but look at the books we have containing the first records of travel in the Highlands: look at the documents we have, showing that the people were starving, and dying of hunger. There is no doubt about it, the people in the past lived most miserably.* ...

This is owing to the altered conditions of living? – *Exactly; they are not satisfied with what their forefathers had forty or fifty years ago, and quite rightly. They have got better houses and a higher standard of living, and would not now be satisfied with what their forefathers had. I don't blame them for it. ... and you cannot get the land for them. It is not there.*

It is perfectly plain from the evidence that crofting had long since ceased to support the population of Knoydart. Neither did deer forests offer much security. Working for wealthy estate owners placed locals in a position of complete economic dependence. They relied on the estate for employment as stalkers, ghillies and domestic servants. This was not a healthy basis for the future and had disastrous consequences in times of retrenchment. Landowners could be unpleasant or benign, tight or spendthrift, and a sporting estate depends upon hunting remaining in fashion. The crofters wished for more land to strengthen their economic position – the proprietor and his agent were determined not to grant it.

Mr Mackay's evidence also allows us to assess whether or not Knoydart could ever support a crofting population. He stated that in order to live 'pretty fairly', a crofter 'should have at least twenty acres of arable land'. According to Morison's survey of 1771 the Barrisdale estate contained a total of about eighty acres of arable. This supported, in 1755, a population of 258. Leaving aside differences and inaccuracies in measurements, and allowing for an average household size of five, the implication of Mackay's estimate is that in 1894 the same land could actually only support twenty people.

Census Data

We also have employment data from the census returns. Figures 6 and 7 summarise the categories for employment in 1841 and 1891. In broad terms it is obvious that the agricultural basis for Knoydart's economy had been badly hit. In 1841 land was held or worked by 146 of Knoydart's population of 928 (15%). In 1891 the corresponding figures were forty-two out of 412 (10%). There is a greater variety of occupations but at least eighteen men are directly dependent upon the estate for employment. It is also striking that in 1891 there were eighteen Paupers. In 1841 the old and weak had been carried by their families. Now they were recognised.

The figures reveal how few trades or crafts were followed locally. This is particularly the case amongst women. Any weaving or spinning was only for home consumption and the lack of craft products made the local population even more dependent upon their proprietor. Virtually all the women in employment in 1891 are described as domestic servants. The number of fishermen was remarkably stable over the period and it was still the case that fifteen men were employed as shepherds. The evidence of Gillies MacKissock in 1894 implies that several of these subsequently lost their jobs.

The Failure to Establish a Fishing Industry

One of the mysteries of Highland history has been the relative failure of West Highlanders to become fishermen. In other parts of the country, the east and north-east coast, Loch Fyne, the Clyde, men turned to fishing and made a success of it. Despite numerous attempts it never took off in the same way in the West Highlands. Lots of reasons have been advanced for this, lack of salt, lack of capital, distance from markets – not all completely persuasive. The Forfeited Estates Commissioners did make valiant, and expensive, attempts to encourage the people of Knoydart to take to fishing, but with no lasting success. In the light of the decline of Highland agriculture this failure to find an alternative means of livelihood seems especially tragic. The sea has long been the Highlands' only bountiful resource.

Fish. – Skate, ling, and cod are to be got along the

Figure 6: Categories of Employment (1841)

Male

Agriculture
Tacksmen	2
Farmers	6
Tenants	5
Crofters	33
Cottars	14
Agricultural Labourers	52
Drover	1

Trade
Merchant	1

Misc
Labourers	9
Male Servants	24
Forester	1
Priest	1
Fox Hunters	2
Rural Constable	1
Ground Officer	1

Fishing
Fishermen	16

Craftsmen
Woollen Weaver	1
Boat Builder	1
Masons	2
Dyker	1
Shoemakers	4
H(ouse) Carpenter	1
Tailor	1

Total 180

Female

Agriculture
Tenant	1
Crofters	6
Cottars	19
Agricultural Labourers	7

Fishing
(Fisherman)	1

Craftswomen
Hand Loom Weavers	2
Wool Spinster	1

Trade
Merchantess	1

Misc
Female Servants	48

Total 86

Total Population 928

Figure 7: Categories of Employment (1891)

Male

Agriculture	
5	Sheep Managers
15	Shepherds
	Misc
1	Farm Grieve
10	Farm Labourers
2	Ploughmen
7	Crofters
1	Cottar

Fishing	
18	Fishermen

Estate	
9	Gamekeepers
2	Wire Fencers
4	Gardeners
1	Coachman
1	Under Groom
1	Butler

Craftsmen	
1	Boatbuilder
6	Joiners
1	Mason
2	Blacksmiths
1	Shoemaker
2	Tailors
1	Hand Loom Weaver
2	Tinkers

Trade 3 / Merchants/Retailers

	Misc
1	Minister
1	Priest
1	Teacher
1	Factor
1	Doctor
1	Police Constable
1	Ferryman
1	Road Contractor
1	Sea Captain
4	Seamen
1	Yacht Master
1	Post Runner
1	Steamboat Agent
1	Annuitant
1	Porter
1	of Private Means
1	Registrar
10	General Labourers
1	Pauper

Total 127

Service 64

	Misc
3	Dressmakers
3	Teachers
1	Cottar
17	Paupers

Total 88

Female — Domestic Servants

Total Population 412

coast of the parish, but sythe or pollock is caught in the greatest abundance, which in summer is chiefly the support of the poor people. The herring-fishing deserves to be particularly mentioned, as in Lochurn they make their appearance so early as July, and continue from that period to the middle of autumn. Here the busses from the the frith of Clyde commonly assemble first, besides a vast number of boats, which croud together from the neighbouring parishes and isles adjacent. It is computed for some years back 30,000 barrels have been annually caught in this loch; but the want of salt prevents the natives from turning to advantage this bounty of Providence, which from their local situation they might otherwise do; at present, they are content with fishing a barrel or two to help the maintenance of their families.

(Reverend Colin Maciver, Minister of Glenelg, 1793)

There is an element of myth about the herring of Loch Hourn, as the following accounts indicate.

In the year 1753 a shoal of herring was left by the tide in the inner Loch Urin [Hourn] above the Skiarries. They were computed at half a mile square from three to five feet deep. All the way down to the Sound of Sky the herring were so thick that, a boat going on the loch, the oars made the herrings fly out of the water like flying fish.

(Archibald Menzies, 1768)

A little farther the loch suddenly turns due South, and has a very narrow inlet to a third reach: this strait is so shallow as to be fordable at the ebb of spring-tides; yet has within, the depth of ten and seventeen fathom: the length is about a mile; the breadth a quarter. About seven years ago [1765] it was so filled with herrings, that had crowded in, that the boats could not force their way, and thousands lay dead on the ebb.

(Thomas Pennant, 1772)

At Loch-Urn, in 1767 or 1768, they came in in such

quantity, that, from the narrows to the very head it was quite full: such a quantity ran on shore, that the beach, for four miles round the head, was covered with them from 6–18" deep ... I am also of opinion that the strongest fish being without, in forcing their way into the inner bay, drove the lightest and weakest on shore. So thick were these last, that they carried before them every other kind of fish they met – even ground-fish, skate, flounders etc. and perished together. They continued at that time several weeks, but not so thick after they had run on shore.

(James Anderson 1785)

In the fishing season it presents a busy and animated appearance, the ground being frequently so well stocked as to afford occupation to three hundred vessels. Two or three years ago a singular occurrence took place, which is mentioned as an instance of the amazing quantity of fish that annually resort hither. A large shoal of herrings were steering boldly up the loch; and as they held their course, though the tide was rapidly falling, they took ground at the head and stranded. The numbers thus left ashore were estimated at the enormous amount of six thousand barrels. For some days the putrid effluvia from such an aggregation of animal substances were intolerably potent, but there were very few inhabitants to be incommoded with this nuisance.

(William Daniell 1819)

No doubt there was such an occasion, but it seems difficult to pin down the year in which it occurred! Certainly the story grew in the telling. Moreover, if Loch Hourn was responsible for something of a myth, so the woods and hills of Knoydart were home to a dark superstition. Pennant writes

in less-enlighten'd times a dreadful spectre haunted these hills, sometimes in form of a great dog, a man, or a thin gigantic hag called Glas-lich.

One problem for the historian is finding reasons for the reluctance of Highlanders to commit themselves to the fishing. This trait comes across in Mr Baird's testimony to the Napier

Commission in 1883.

Do they fish much? – *Some of them fish.*

Do they prosecute it with any vigour? – *Not so much as I should like. I had a good deal of annoyance with them some years ago. I was very much annoyed at their not fishing, and I called the heads of the families together one day, and rather abused them for allowing the east coast fishers to come and take the fish away under their noses. They lie between Loch Hourn and Loch Nevis, and Loch Hourn has been a large fishing station of late. I asked why they stood by with their hands folded, when they saw the east coast men taking the food from under their noses? They explained that their only difficulty was the want of nets. I asked how much it would cost to supply them with nets. I was told about £15 for each boat, and the men there represented half a dozen boats. They were overjoyed when I told them I would furnish them with the money if they would repay me in a reasonable time. They said they would repay me in three months. I said that three years would do quite well. They went away quite overjoyed. When I came back next year I found that one man had purchased £5 worth of nets from a neighbour, but otherwise the offer had not been taken advantage of at all. I had told them they were to get nets, and my factor was entrusted to pay for them as soon as they were bought, and all they had to do was to send the bill to me....*

Did they make much last year at the herring fishing? – *Very little I think.*

Was that owing to their own fault? – *I can understand no other cause for it.*

It was a very good fishing last year? – *I have been so informed. I was making some inquiry last winter, and I was told there was something like £180,000 worth of herring taken out of Loch Hourn.*

Mr Baird's remonstrations must have had some effect because in 1885 he spent over £83 supplying several of the crofters with fishing nets. Unfortunately, despite investment by the Forfeited

Estates Commissioners, despite the generosity of Mr Baird, despite the huge shoals of herring, a fishing industry failed to take root locally. Unlike the Dutch before them, the men of the Clyde or the East Coasters, the people of Knoydart failed to capitalise on just about their only plentiful natural resource. They were not alone. The same happened along much of the west coast and the reasons are still a matter of debate.

Mr Mackay gave his opinions on the subject to the Deer Forest Commission in 1894.

But if they had greater facilities of disposing of the fish when caught, such as they look to, – e.g., if the Mallaig railway were finished, don't you think they would fish? – *I don't think they would and I don't think they ever did.*

You think that the west coast people are quite unfit for fishing? – *No, no, I don't think so; but I think they would be very much better fishermen if they had no crofts at all. If they were exclusively fishermen, they would make capital fishermen, but they are a blend between the crofter and the fishermen, and the result is that they do not work either of these occupations to advantage.*

The evidence from the Census Returns

There is other evidence we can extract from the Census Returns which gives us insights into the lives and conditions of people in Knoydart. (*See* Figure 4).

Each house was usually occupied by only one family. Given short life expectancy it was common to find grandparents and other relations sharing the same roof but the nuclear family unit was the norm. In the case of large families the younger children often seem to have been farmed out amongst relatives. Average household size was never more than six and until late in the nineteenth century most houses were physically small.

There were generally more women than men. This is particularly true in 1851 when the proportion was 4 men to every 5 women. There are naturally more male births than female but over a lifetime things tend to balance out as more males die young. It is difficult to know quite what forces were at work in Knoydart but there were significantly fewer males than females. This was most acute above the age of fifty when the proportion in both 1851 and 1861 was 1:2. Most people died young – but men died younger.

The age structure was similar to that of a developing country today. Lots of children were born; adults aged early and died young. In 1851, over half the total population was under 20, as it had been in 1755. Only 4% lived to more than seventy years old. This meant that Knoydart had a high proportion of young women, could multiply rapidly, and did not have to support many elderly dependents.

By the end of the nineteenth century, average household size had declined markedly which must have meant some improvement in living standards. At the same time houses were improving in size and quality. We can use the number of windowed rooms as an indicator of housing standards. In 1861 each house had an average of 2.7 windowed rooms, by 1891 this average had risen to 4.2. No doubt, improved living conditions had a beneficial effect on health and longevity.

There were over fifty different surnames in 1851, mainly Highland, although some were variant spellings of others. Macdonald and Macdonell (the same name although spelled differently) formed by far the largest group – over 37% of the total. The eight most common surnames – Macdonald, Mackinnon, Macpherson, Cameron, Kennedy, Macdougall, Maclellan and Campbell – together account for over 71% of all names.

It is the same with forenames. Among females, the names Ann, Catherine, Christina, Mary and Margaret account for two-thirds of all the names in Knoydart in 1851 and 1861. There was slightly less uniformity amongst males, but in 1851 the five names of Angus, Alexander, Archibald, Donald and John made up over 60% of the total.

It is quite extraordinary how few outsiders lived in Knoydart. In 1851, 89% of Knoydart residents were born in Inverness-shire, the vast majority of them being born in Glenelg parish – which usually meant Knoydart. There had been some immigration, particularly from Skye (over 5% of the total population), but also from Morar, Arisaig and Kilmonivaig. There was only

one immigrant from outside Scotland and very few from the
Lowlands – the largest group being twelve people from Dumfries.

What conclusions can we draw from this mass of raw data?
What is striking is the degree of uniformity and homogeneity in
Knoydart society. Britain today is often described as
multicultural. We have a mix of races, colours and creeds.
Individuals express their differences. Knoydart in the mid-
nineteenth century was the precise opposite. It was an
extraordinarily homogenous society in which virtually everybody
had been born locally and shared the same religion and beliefs.
People tended to share the same surnames and Christian names;
they were born in Glenelg Parish, Inverness-shire, and they
followed similar sorts of occupations. As the nineteenth century
progressed, changes began to take place but the local social fabric
was still largely intact. Unfortunately, the removal of its
economic base meant it was only a matter of time before it
disintegrated and dispersed.

Failure

The failure of Highland society to develop new economic forms
can be seen as a product of its history. The Highlander had grown
dependent upon his landholding, theft was denied him, and
the agricultural potential of areas like Knoydart was an
insufficient base. Other societies came to rely on the sea, which,
for all its savagery, offered a richer living. The land of Knoydart
simply could not sustain a population into the twentieth century,
and its occupants failed to find an alternative. Not all
nineteenth-century observers were sympathetic to Highlanders
and their economic problems, but it is idle to blame them for
this failure to adjust. Their helplessness may have exasperated
some contemporaries but over the generations they had been
so ground down by poverty that they had no capital but their
labour. In a rural environment they could not easily organise or
combine. Their wealthier members had emigrated towards the
end of the eighteenth century. Those who remained were
economically, politically and legally depressed.

This trend is clearly seen in the second half of the nineteenth
century. The culture of dependence did not just occur; it grew,
over a period of time. The people of Knoydart became dependent

after many years of struggle against the landscape, the climate and the landowner. The potato blight of 1846 and the Clearance of 1853 must have been traumatic for their sense of self-esteem. Their pride had to be swallowed for the sake of their children; they must earn whatever way they could. Their lack of capital meant they could not escape from the poverty trap; the social and economic structures meant they had no political power; their future lay in the hands of the landowners. Once their labour was no longer required in Knoydart they had to take themselves to where it was valued, outwith the Highland area. Few would have understood why they were such victims of circumstance. Understanding their situation was irrelevant for most; they were faced with a simple choice: stay or go. The people have largely gone; the land remains, slowly swallowing their signs of occupation.

Geography and history have been harsh to Knoydart, they have emptied the landscape. In a way this is an honest verdict on the Highlander's struggle with his environment. Writing in 1887, when Knoydart still had over 400 people, Fraser-Mackintosh said:

> The times, indeed, are changed in 'the country' of Knoydart, as its people loved to designate it. No longer shall such as the gay and dashing, but extravagant, Eneas-Scotus ... accompanied by a noisy and merry band of followers, together with his deerhounds ... his slowhounds ... his mongrels ... his terriers ... be seen ranging over 'the country', eagerly engaged in 'hunting the fox'. No longer does a Glengarry, with a numerous retinue ... hold high festival in Glendulochan. No longer shall the shepherd or herd-boy, overpowered by sleep after his mid-day repast, awake in trembling, to find the noontide hag, 'Glas-lich', glaring upon him with fixed and malevolent eye, whose hated presence can only be ridded by invocation and the sign of the cross. Yes, these are gone; the ancient peoples are gone. But the mountains, the streams, the lakes, remain.

The population is now a fraction of the total in 1887, and Fraser-Mackintosh's words ring ever more true. It is the landscape

that is Knoydart now, for the land is longer than men and, in
the end, the land resumes.

Chapter 11

KNOYDART IN THE TWENTIETH CENTURY

The Land Issue

The issue of who owns the land has remained of critical importance to Knoydart in the twentieth century. In order to understand the nature of this problem it must be placed in its longer historical context. For perhaps 800 years Knoydart was owned as a unit. Although cadet families were locally important, it belonged to Clanranald and then Glengarry as a distinct and recognizable entity until 1857. It passed, as a unit, into the hands of the Bairds, the Bowlbys and the Brockets, and it is only recently that it has begun to fragment. The legitimacy of ownership is lost in the murky politics of the Middle Ages where right was merely power. Chiefs inherited by succession, and their landholdings, first established and maintained by the sword, gradually became recognized in law.

Some have argued for a democratic element in the clan system and it is true that occasionally the succession did not pass down the direct line but devolved to one who was regarded as more likely to maintain the clan's position. However, it would be a travesty to regard the clan as anything other than hierarchical, and succession eventually resolved into primogeniture, regardless of suitability. This custom was reinforced by the structure and process of Scots law and so, whatever may have been the medieval role of the clan chief, by the nineteenth century he was simply the landowner. Any identity of purpose between chief and clan fell apart in the eighteenth century, if not much earlier. There were a few honourable exceptions and some tacksmen chose to emigrate with their people rather than remain at home in an economic and social framework in which they felt alien. As John Macdonald of Glenaladale wrote in 1772:

> Emigrations are like to demolish the Highland Lairds, and very deservedly.

It was no longer necessary for chief and clansmen to share economic interests, and as it turned out they seldom did. It took time for the enormous body of cultural support for the landlords as clan chiefs to evaporate. But, by the late nineteenth century when landowners were often unconnected with any clan, there was already a yawning social chasm between tenant and landowner.

Lacking any economic sympathy with their tenants, and shorn of their military functions after Culloden, the chiefs set about realising their assets. By long-lived cultural tradition they had a grandiose view of their own status and the style they should maintain. Many engaged in high living and ran up enormous debts. Rents in kind were transformed into cash and then raised exorbitantly. If tenants could not, or would not, pay then Lowland sheep farmers were brought in who would. As cattle declined in relative importance so the Highland pastoral system became dangerously lop-sided. The heavy grazing of sheep proved to have damaging ecological side-effects whilst the practice of muirburn checked any natural regeneration of woodland.

Between 1750 and 1850 crucial economic opportunities were missed. Fortunes were made from the kelp trade during the Napoleonic wars but unfortunately this industry rose and fell without any enduring benefit to the Highlands. Because of their position of economic power we can hold landowners partly responsible for this, but it is less easy to blame them for the failure to develop the fishing industry. It remains one of the mysteries of Highland history as to why the people of the west coast did not turn to fishing more than they did. It may be that it was partly due to their very rootedness in the land. Certainly some contemporary commentators thought so. Cattle droving was a mainstay of the Highland economy for centuries but prices dropped dramatically after the Napoleonic wars and the trade declined in relative importance.

The much vaunted community of interest between chief and clan was conspicuous by its absence after Culloden. Landowners, whether clan chief or no, could be extraordinarily selfish in pursuing their own interests regardless of their clansmen or tenants. James Hunter has demonstrated how they alternately supported or discouraged emigration as it suited their own purposes. Absenteeism undoubtedly contributed to a sense of alienation on the part of both landlord and tenant. A huge gap of understanding, and therefore sympathy, developed between the two sides.

This disjunction was worsened by the increasing polarisation of society. Many of the intermediate members – the tacksmen, the redeemed wadsetters, the cadet families and small farmers – left during the late eighteenth century, taking their money and their enterprise with them. Spanish John sailed from Knoydart on the *Pearl* in 1773, as did the family of Ardnaslishnish. In 1786 the exodus was even more emphatic. There is copious evidence that these early emigrants were not the poorest members of society, but those with a little capital. Expectations were rising, families were no longer content with what the old world had to offer. There is no doubt that many people were pulled to the New World just as others were pushed. At home, there was a widening gulf between the landlord, who owned everything, and the crofters and cottars, who had little or nothing. The trauma of the Clearances only served to increase this sense of alienation.

These were the difficulties generated by the Highland situation, the history and economy of Highland society as it had developed since the Middle Ages. But there were other more general factors at work for which we can assign no blame to a particular interest or group. Of these, undoubtedly the most important was a rapidly expanding population. Whether due to more food, inoculation, or better healthcare, hygiene and living standards, this trend upset any economic equilibrium in the Highlands. The traditional solution of theft from the Lowlands or Ireland was no longer available, whilst improved communications meant the outside world became more aware of Highland problems.

The Highlands offered very few economic opportunities to sustain its growing population. The area had always been scarce of natural resources. Agriculture was perpetually struggling against an adverse climate, while cattle and corn prices were dependent on factors outwith Highland control. The fishing industry was underdeveloped and volatile, whilst the forests were exploited without being replaced. There began a long period of relative decline. Wealth was not retained within the region, what was generated locally was all too often taken or spent abroad. There was a widening gulf between rich and poor and increasing dependence on the landowner for employment.

Even with a benevolent landlord it became impossible for the traditional methods to sustain the population of the Highlands. This was not so much because of changes in the Highlands as changes that were taking place elsewhere. Britain became urban and industrial, its economic structure based first on manufacturing and, more recently, on service industries. The motors and pace of change were set in the industrial cities of the south. The speed of communications and transport have tied us into a global economic system and it is not yet apparent where the Highlands are to find their niche. The Highland economy depended primarily on pastoral farming, and this may have gone forever. The economic trends provoked by industrialisation were so powerful, so compelling, that for two centuries they have wreaked havoc in Highland and many other societies. All countries have experienced demographic, social and cultural changes as adjustments are made to their economic base. In Britain, the Highland area has suffered more than most.

Landlordism: The Economic and Moral Arguments

Highlanders have for so long been the victims of change that it is practically impossible to read a history of the Highlands without meeting blame. It is morally satisfactory for historians to assign blame and there is certainly no shortage of cause in the last two centuries, but against the ineluctable march of economic history the question of responsibility and blame is practically irrelevant. From an external viewpoint, the evils and inadequacies of Highland landlords are almost incidental when seen against the enormous economic changes that have swept Britain in the last 250 years. Highland society has been helpless and hapless, responding to events elsewhere, dwarfed by the mighty economic structures of industrial Britain. Until 1746, its high relative manpower made the Highlands an important and distinct unit. Since then, it has become an impoverished and impotent appendage.

From a Highland perspective, and within a Highland context, the nature of landlordism is extremely important. As a historical and cultural phenomenon it is much more important here than elsewhere in Britain where the levers of economic power passed to the mercantile and industrial barons. Because of its obvious evils, because of the long history of clearance and exploitation, it is tempting to say that landlordism is economically bad. However, it is difficult to sustain this argument in the late nineteenth and twentieth centuries. There is no doubt that a great many Highland estates have been dependent on charitable landowners for upwards of a century. The economic pros and cons of landlordism are too complex for a glib indictment.

When discussing the problems of landlordism in Scotland – as in Knoydart in 1948 – a lot of attention is devoted to the personal characteristics of the landlord. Such arguments serve to increase our sense of moral outrage and marshal support for a political cause, but strictly speaking the characteristics of particular landlords should be irrelevant when making objective judgements about the nature of landlordism. Over the last two centuries there have been a great variety of Highland landlords. These have ranged from callous despots who cared not a jot for their tenantry to those who have taken themselves to the point of ruin to help their people. They have been present or absent, Highland or Lowland, Scottish or English, and now, increasingly, from abroad.

People are naturally conservative, and rural society does not take easily to revolutionary change. Accordingly, there have been many apologists for landlords from within the Highlands, particularly if they happen to be the clan chief. Frequently the factor gets the blame – the landlord would have rectified the situation, if only he had known about it. Much of this is special pleading. If you accept the right of individuals to own huge estates in the Highlands then you must accept bad owners as well as good. You may hope for benevolent patriarchs, you may get a malevolent reactionary. Moreover, in times of general economic difficulty, even the most benign patrician may be forced to take measures his tenantry find unpalatable. We can understand the bitterness and rancour of Highland tenants in a period of great change. An economic system that had supported most of them, with ups and downs, for thousands of years, was now failing them. Or rather, it was not enabling them to provide the rents their landlords expected, feed their expanding families, or meet their own rising expectations.

Few Highlanders had any educational opportunities, few had travelled widely or had any understanding of the changes taking place throughout Highland society. They looked to their leaders in this new situation, and their leaders largely betrayed them. In a hierarchical society, as the Highlands always were, it was up to the rich and powerful to lead their clan. Unfortunately, few Highland chieftains had the foresight or ability to try and adapt their people to changed circumstances. Much has been said about the kindred-based structures of Highland society. It is not obvious that such considerations were at the forefront of the minds of most Highland chiefs as they struggled with the changing economic realities of Britain. What was needed was a little self-discipline, some deferred gratification. The very nature of Highland society precluded this. It was incumbent on the chief to consume conspicuously, to display magnificently, to hunt ostentatiously, to vaunt, to boast, to squander. Their bards, their poets, their cultural and historical traditions all pushed them one way. They were ill-served by the bankers and lawyers who either did not warn them of the perils ahead, who warned them and were not heeded, or who simply fleeced them.

We are left with the moral argument alone. Landlordism can only be condemned unequivocally on moral grounds. Landlordism is bad, even when it is good – it is wrong for the land to be in the hands of one man. The irony at the present time is that, whilst we can argue that landlordism is morally iniquitous, it may be economically beneficial. This is not a satisfactory paradox but we must recognize that a great many Highland estates currently survive because wealthy individuals are prepared to run them either at a loss or at paltry rates of return. This implies that the really critical issue today is not ownership, but subsidy. Is ownership incidental then? Certainly not to those who suffer under bad landlords, and not in the context of who is to be subsidised for doing what. There is also the argument that this type of ownership and control over resources serves to stifle local enterprise and diversity. It is against this background that we should see the land raid of 1948 and the continuing debate over land ownership and usage.

1948 Land Raid

From 1893 to the 1930s, Knoydart was owned by the Bowlby family. Retrospectively this is cast as a halcyon period. Shooting parties came and went, there were big social functions and balls, there was employment. This rosy view may not bear historical scrutiny since the population of the area declined from 412 in 1891 to about 80 in 1947. The underlying economic negatives were still at work. The Bowlbys were remembered as benevolent proprietors but, in the early 1930s, they sold the estate to the Brockets. In the subsequent dispute, opinions became sharply polarised and in the process of political argument all sorts of accusations, some relevant, some not, flew about.

Lord Brocket comes across as a deeply unsympathetic character. He, along with a number of other figures from the British Establishment, was a keen supporter of what Hitler was then doing in Germany. He and his wife earned an unfortunate reputation locally for their obsession with privacy. This applied not only to visitors to Knoydart, but even to local children who were banned from the beach in front of the Big House. Strictly speaking, of course, these personal shortcomings are irrelevant to the economic argument, although they undoubtedly flavoured the moral indignation of the local population and swelled the sympathy from elsewhere.

More importantly, locals were convinced that Brocket was trying to run down the estate as a farming unit and was really only interested in preserving it as an exclusive sporting estate. Since this threatened their jobs and livelihoods, and indeed their continued presence on the peninsula, they naturally viewed him with a great deal of suspicion. Elderly employees were paid off and there was a deep pessimism about the continued security of the local community. On the other hand, Lord Brocket claimed in 1948 that his annual wage bill was £6000, which implied that he was subsidising local jobs.

After World War II, locals felt that Brocket was deliberately blocking every proposal for improvement. They suspected his motives and found an articulate spokesman in the young parish priest, Reverend Colin Macpherson. Approaches to the Department of Agriculture for division of the estate into smallholdings met with acknowledgement but nothing more. It was felt that nothing would succeed except dramatic action and so a group of local men decided to emulate the tactics of the land-raid as adopted by the Land League in the late nineteenth century. Their subsequent actions earned them the title of 'The Seven Men of Knoydart'.

On 9 November 1948 these local men staked claims to land on the Kilchoan and Scottos farms. Lord Brocket applied immediately to the Court of Session for an Interim Interdict – with success. The men did not defy this interdict and adopted the strictly legal course of defending their actions through a solicitor. (In retrospect some of them felt that this was their fatal mistake). Answers to the interdict were lodged in court, while the Department of Agriculture put forward a scheme for a number of separate holdings. Arthur Woodburn, Labour Secretary of State for Scotland, decided instead to commission a survey by John Cameron, a hill farmer from Perthshire, whose brief was

> to advise on the best means of securing the full develop-
> ment of the resources of the area, taking into account
> the social, economic and financial issues involved.

A public hearing was held in Mallaig on 22 December 1948 at which lawyers for both sides argued their case amidst a great deal of press coverage. In early 1949 John Cameron reported – against the Seven Men of Knoydart. Mr Cameron has come in for a good deal of criticism over the years so it is only fair to give his reasons in detail. He wrote:

> The division of this type of country into units, i.e. separate
> economic hill herdings, has almost insuperable difficulties
> in respect of the provision and location of homes and

homesteads with even a minimum of arable or inbye land in necessary proximity to the herding, the provision of separate sheep-handling equipment, roads and fencing serving only a single unit and in the end creating in many instances an isolated home and also in respect to the building up of the stock.

Considering the previously much higher population of Knoydart, he argued

That population, however, was largely along the coast and relied very much on sea fishing for a livelihood. Whatever be the cause, this type of sea fishing has failed and cannot now support what is known as the 'fishing croft'. Further, the standard of living of the larger population ... is not one which could be acceptable to-day.

His conclusions were:

I do not recommend development as separate units on the lines broadly indicated in the Department of Agriculture for Scotland Scheme featuring 19 holdings, nor under the Father Macpherson Scheme featuring 40 holdings.

In addition to the practical reasons already referred to, cost would be out of proportion to production results, and the livelihood would be certainly insecure and with little comfort. Further, nothing emerged at the Mallaig meeting to show that men of the type, skilled hill men, essential in my opinion to the success of such holdings, are among the lists of applicants....

I recommend development as a single unit under one direction, preferably with a limited forestry development to be undertaken by the Estate.

However, Mr Cameron recognised that the estate might not fulfil its obligations and added

If at the end of ten years stock raising has not maintained the stocking target and has not given an annual output commensurate with the stocking numbers, I recommend a review of the position, particularly with a view to the

Forestry Commission acquiring the property under the Forestry Act, 1945.

He finished:

> I regret the nature of my report, as I am well aware that the natural instinct of Highlanders is to have their own individual holdings, both for cultivation and the raising of stock, rather than for wage-earning employment, whether in agriculture or forestry, but I cannot see that it would be in their interests to recommend the development of such holdings in Knoydart.

Some put the contrary view that Cameron had concentrated purely on the economic factors and ignored the social arguments, but this was to no effect. The Secretary of State accepted the Cameron Report and the Land Raid was over. Within a few years Brocket had sold up and today the estate population is composed of incomers. It is ironic that, in 1948, it was felt it should be run as a single unit when now it has been broken up by market forces.

The decision against the Land Raiders has met with a good deal of criticism. At the time there was a dissenting opinion that

> there was no hope of development in the Highlands unless the State was prepared to invest a good deal of money for such purposes.
>
> MacDougall, A. (1993)
> *Knoydart*

This though is the crux of the matter. There is seldom an economic argument for investment in the Highlands. Some argue for governments to take a more proactive, interventionist approach for social reasons. At the end of the twentieth century governments are less interested in public spending and appear quite happy to let market forces operate as they will.

There was enormous sympathy for the Seven Men of Knoydart at the time. Support was voiced all over Scotland and funds flowed in for their legal action. In retrospect, they were right about one thing, unless they secured legal tenure in Knoydart their future was doomed. They have all gone. But we must look past the sympathy they received and the politicisation of the argument and ask whether John Cameron was not right as well. Expectations have risen enormously since 1948 and the economic fundamentals are working ever more strongly against Highland agriculture. We are now a long way from World War II and the political need to boost domestic food production regardless of cost. Subsidies to farmers are increasingly questioned. The Seven Men of Knoydart were right, but so perhaps was John Cameron; their future could not be sustained without subsidy. Even at the time otherwise sympathetic locals expressed their doubts about whether the land raiders could make a go of it. Public money should always be subject to scrutiny and we can hardly blame John Cameron for his scepticism.

To the individual occupants of a Highland estate the issue of landlordism is central, from the viewpoint of government it is almost incidental. There are few votes at issue, potentially a lot of money, and it is peripheral to the concerns of most of the electorate. It is a relic of history, a problem that has never been tackled. In the drained and exhausted Britain of 1948 it is understandable that subsidising a Highland estate, however badly run, was not a high priority. From the perspective of the small number of people in Knoydart their future was doomed because of the unpleasant nature of one bad landlord. And yet nobody can *expect* to be subsidized, whether by landlord or government. As one of the Land Raiders, Archie Macdougall, later said, they had 'tried so hard to find a way to stay in the place they loved'. This sentence could stand as an epitaph on the struggle between economic fact and natural beauty that has torn at men's hearts for the last two centuries in Knoydart.

Land Reform

Knoydart's history, in particular the 1853 Clearance and the 1948 Land Raid, has added an emotional intensity to the continuing debate on land reform. Unfortunately these two cathartic events have overshadowed the slow process of economic decline and emigration that has been going on since 1773. Land ownership is perceived by some as the critical issue in Knoydart and other parts of the Highlands. This is partly because land has been the only avenue of economic opportunity. Lacking burghs, factories, mines and commerce, subject to the vagaries of the herring, land was what underpinned a Highlander's economic outlook. So the issue of who owned the land has always appeared fundamental. This view has been reinforced by the experience of history. The trauma and abuse of the Clearances have left the conviction that unless the land is controlled by the community then Highlanders are not safe. Of course no community can guarantee safety from change, but Highland communities are particularly vulnerable since they lack economic alternatives.

So, for perfectly understandable reasons, community ownership is now held up as the ideal in a Highland context. Unfortunately this only solves the problem of ownership, not that of usage. Community ownership does not necessarily mean prosperity. It is doubtful if Highland agriculture can ever sustain significant numbers of people. If private landowners are currently subsidising the Highlands then what is going to replace them under community ownership? It will involve public money both to buy the land in the first place and sustain a population on it thereafter. It is difficult to see any government taking on such a commitment, except in isolated cases. Moreover, with all governments adopting a capitalist perspective, such communities would, sooner or later, be expected to become economically viable.

The Highlands are simply too fragile an environment for the operation of laissez-faire capitalism. If we apply free-market conditions then allowing sheep to ravage the hillsides for nearly two centuries was in fact the 'best' use of the land, as was chopping down the trees for ironworks and scooping all the herring from the sea lochs. The resources of the Highlands are so scarce and slow to regenerate, the economic opportunities so scant, the ecological balance so fragile, that it is not a sufficiently robust arena in which to let capitalism rage unchecked.

It is arguable that the Highland area is so damaged and weakened that what is now required is not the free play of market forces but planning, regulation and state intervention; with all their trappings of bureaucracy, inefficiency and expense. Unfortunately this runs against the tide of government thinking for the last twenty years, which has opted instead to give market forces free rein. Is there a better future for the Highlands in letting individual enterprise run its course; or is it the case that only within an integrated framework of forestry, fishing and land reform that long-term economic redemption can be won?

The argument for intervention can also be applied to the issue of land-ownership. One of the problems facing land-reform in a Highland context is that land has an artificially high value. This reflects its beauty, its romance, its promise of privacy, rather than any economic opportunities it offers. In economic terms it seldom gives an attractive return on the capital employed in its purchase. A Highland estate is often simply a bolt-hole for the rich. The Highlands share this problem with other parts of Britain but it does offer an argument for tying land-valuations to an independent assessment of their economic worth as opposed to their free-market value. This, however, requires government intervention.

The future

There are two distinct issues in any debate about the future of the Highlands, landlordism and subsidy, and it is often the case that one overshadows the other. Attention is always drawn to the politics of clearance and ownership, and not to the underlying economics. However, as a result of recent highly-publicised events in Knoydart and elsewhere, the problems of landlordism are back in the limelight. Sometimes it is abuse, sometimes it is neglect, but either way the levers of legal and economic power are concentrated in the hands of one person. Instead of diversity and pluralism there are economic and political monoliths, sometimes benevolent, sometimes not. Some observers feel regret when the great estates are broken up, others argue that it can free up enterprise and innovation.

The other problem is subsidy. Regardless of the issue of landlordism, should the Highlands be subsidised? If we can imagine the alternative of no landlords then would Highlanders deserve subsidy in order to sustain life in an environment which, under free market conditions, could actually only support tiny numbers of people? Cast in this light we have further dilemmas. How can we sustain economic life in an area where resources are so poor and the traditional methods of earning a living have been left behind by the pace of economic change? If we remove animal subsidies, development boards, conservation groups, wildlife officers, and the various other quangoes and charities that currently occupy and support much of the Highlands then who and what would be left?

In terms of its sporting income or agricultural value, Knoydart could probably not sustain more than a handful of people. Even then any infrastructure of public service and care would have to be heavily subsidised. Perpetual subsidy is not an option politicians face, let alone accept. How is it going to be possible to make Knoydart economically viable? If it is not, and perhaps never will be, then even facing up to this issue is problematic because of its implications for the whole Highland area. Few have addressed these dilemmas. Nobody dare either advocate clearance or admit perpetual subsidy, and so we stagger from one stop-gap measure to another. There is no coherent policy for Highland development. It is safer and more convenient to divert attention towards the abuses which undoubtedly existed in the past and which persist in some areas today. Current political debate often concentrates on the business of assigning blame, rather than clear-cut, concrete proposals about who should do what for the future.

These problems have been compounded by a certain ossification of the legal structures. Both landowners and crofters have legal rights that were established under different social and economic orders. It is arguable that neither are really suited to today's economic and social requirements. In a world of fluid capital, of constantly changing employment patterns, these old-established legal rights can appear either as anchors of stability in a sea of change, or as so much deadwood hampering the adaptation of Highland society to the demands of a modern economy.

It is still possible to take an optimistic view of the future. Highlanders have come this far and survived. Not all areas are deserted. Scotland is rich enough to embark on some regeneration; to restore some life to the area, as opposed to just preserving it. There must be a long process of repair. There cannot be an economic argument for investment in the Highlands, there will be no return for generations. The damage to the Highland landscape and woodland could take a century to make good. The problem is to devise sustainable economic forms that do not depend on subsidy, to marry communal aspirations with individual endeavour. Ideally the enterprise of capitalism would be regulated in order to prevent the exploitation of such a fragile environment. Unfortunately market forces and sustainable development will always pull in different directions.

EPILOGUE

Until the eighteenth century, it was possible to sustain life in Knoydart. There were few frills and no riches; poverty was the norm, starvation was frequent – deferred by predation or resolved by death. A population hovered, not much above subsistence level, with little by way of a substantial material culture. They left scant traces above ground, no fine buildings, painting or architecture. There are a few carved stones, some phrases in poetry and song, some notions in language, all but gone. Their presence just resonates in old documents and through the rigs, dykes and lazybeds of their long-abandoned farms. The old history remains – fossilised in the landscape, in the place-names, in worn old papers and plans, in the stories of poverty and failure, in the anguish and sympathy of Donald Ross, in the pride and stoicism of Charles Macdonald in his blue bonnet, in the frustration and anger of the Seven Men of Knoydart. We cannot bring it back in body, but we can bring it to mind where it will enjoy some form of life. That is history. We cannot resuscitate it, but we can remember.

The truth is that it has not been possible, probably since about 1700, to sustain the population of Knoydart without subsidy. Before this the surplus people starved or stole. From the 1730s, theft was practised on a grand scale by Barrisdale, followed by blackmail. After 1755 there was a relatively benign interlude for the Barrisdale estate until 1784. The Forfeited Estates Commissioners struggled to introduce the brave new world of improved agriculture, without perhaps ever realising that the fundamentals were against them. The climate, the soil, the landscape, all militated against farming. Since about 1770 the disjunction between resources and need, between income and expectation, has resulted in debt, hunger, emigration, clearance or subsidy.

Cattle had always been the backbone of the Highland pastoral economy, but after 1820 their prices collapsed. For a time sheep swept all before them. Scottos had been cleared in 1784. The better-off tenants emigrated in 1786 whilst the poorer probably went to swell the western coastal settlements between Inverguseran and Sandaig. These, in turn, were grossly overpopulated by 1841. Sheep came and went, only to be replaced by deer forests requiring even less human management. Once the agricultural base had collapsed what else was there? There were no towns to absorb the surplus population, no factories to take up the cheap labour. The fishing industry did not develop as it did in North Morar.

Knoydart's fundamental problem was always economic, how to support a population except by agriculture – in an area where weather and relief are hostile. Before the eighteenth century, the alternatives were simple. The population starved, or they stole. After Culloden the political framework changed and neither of these options were acceptable. Landowners and the public conscience have wrestled with the problems since. Owners have come and gone. In fact, Knoydart has been owned by more families in the last century than in the previous seven. At best, private owners can be benevolently paternal, digging into their own pockets to sustain themselves and their servants in uneconomic life-forms. At worst, they can be tyrannical. Knoydart has had a variety of owners, some well-meaning, some less so. Schemes and proposals have come and gone. There has been fishing and stalking, forestry, sheep farming, adventure schools, tourism. By themselves none of these is the complete answer; it is not even certain that a combination of them would be sufficient without a degree of public subsidy.

The old history of Knoydart is over. An old way of life, defined partly by language, partly by its relationship with soil and sea, is gone. It can never be resuscitated. What we have now in Knoydart, as in other parts of the Highlands, are new modes of living, new forms of economic life, new attempts to overcome the old adversities of distance, desolation and climate.

It is all very well for the historian to bewail the iniquities of the past. Much that happened in Knoydart was brutal and cold-blooded. But when all is said and done, when every cruelty has been recounted, every petty tyranny revealed, when the sheep have been cursed and the landowners condemned, we must still face the issue squarely. How do you make a living – a real, honest, profitable, unsubsidized living – in a remote corner of the Highlands in the new millennium? The Knoydart that existed in all previous history has gone, the indigenous inhabitants entirely dispersed. In a way, that is a sound historical judgement on what is possible in remote areas, given their harshness and our ever-increasing expectations. Maybe the best we can currently do for Knoydart is keep it afloat with public subsidy, allow the rich and charitable to buy and build holiday homes, plant trees and cosset wildlife.

History is always human history, and in the context of Knoydart several thousand years of history ended imperceptibly. Knoydart could not sustain the traditional modes of living, could not find alternatives, and the people drained away. What happens now is a new start, a new challenge. However the mountains, the rivers, the lochs remain. Humans are as engrossed with them as ever, but for different reasons. They are no longer adversaries in a struggle for life. They are companions, or challenges, romantic views or nostalgic dreams. To the aura of natural beauty is now added the lure of a vanished culture – and a sense of tragedy.

Each reader of the past, whether in document or landscape, each observer of a ruin or lazybed, of a march dyke, a cleared field or beach, can tell something of its history, conjure something of its noise; can wonder at the strength of purpose, the tenacity, the stubbornness of those Gaels who, for hundreds of years, struggled through their short and desperate lives, dependent on their cattle, shellfish, herring, peat; struggled to transmit a language and a culture to yet another short-lived generation, until the day when a richer, leisured people would wonder at, and attempt to record, the shadow of their story.

READING LIST

This is not a complete bibliography – but a list of suggestions for further reading.

Blundell, O. (1917) *Catholic Highlands of Scotland*, Edinburgh

Bumsted, J. M. (1982) *The People's Clearance*, Edinburgh

Fraser-Mackintosh, C. (1897) *Antiquarian Notes*, Inverness

Grigor, I. F. (1980) 'The Seven Men of Knoydart', in: Kay, W. (ed.), *Odyssey*, Edinburgh

Henderson, I. (1970) 'North Pictland, Appendix A', in *The Dark Ages in the Highlands*, Inverness Field Club, Inverness

Hunter, J. (1976) *The Making of the Crofting Community*, John Donald, Edinburgh

Macdonald, A and Macdonald, A. (1896, 1900, 1904) *Clan Donald, Vols. I-III*, Inverness

Macdonald, A and Macdonald, A. (1924) *The Poems of Alexander Macdonald*, Inverness

Macdonald, C. (1997) *Moidart, Among the Clanranalds*, Birlinn, Edinburgh

Macdonald, N. H. (1979) *The Clan Ranald of Knoydart and Glen*garry, Edinburgh

Macdonell, J. (1931) *Spanish John*, Blackwood, Edinburgh

MacDougall, A. (1993) *Knoydart, The Last Scottish Land Raid*, Lyndhurst

Mclean, M. (1991) *The People of Glengarry*, McGill–Queen's University Press, Montreal

Millar, A. H. (1909) *Forfeited Estates Papers*, Scottish History Society, Edinburgh

Mitchell, A. (ed.) (1907) *Macfarlane's Geographical Collections*, *Vol II*, Scottish History Society, Edinburgh

Munro, R. W. (1984) *Taming the Rough Bounds*, Society of West Highland and Island Historical Research, Coll

Prebble, J. (1969) *The Highland Clearances*, Harmondsworth

Ross, D. (1853) *The Glengarry Evictions*, Glasgow

Smith, A. M. (1982) *Jacobite Estates of the Forty-five*, John Donald, Edinburgh

Starmore, G. (1980) 'The Knoydart Alternative', in *North 7*, Inverness

Stone, J. (1991) *Illustrated Maps of Scotland*, Studio Editions, London

Stone, J. (1989) *The Pont Manuscript Maps of Scotland*, Map Collector Publications, Tring

Thomson, D. S. (1960–63) 'The Macmhuirich Bardic Family', in *Transactions of the Gaelic Society of Inverness XLIII*

Watson, W. J. (ed.) (1978) *Scottish Verse from the Book of the Dean of Lismore*, Scottish Gaelic Texts Society, Scottish Academic Press, Edinburgh

Wills, V. (ed.) (1973) *Reports on the Annexed Estates*, Edinburgh